Praise for Baconish

"If you are in the 'bacon makes everything better' crowd, but you don't eat animals or you just don't want the cholesterol, you'll love this brilliant new cookbook. Learn to make ten kinds of vegetable-based bacon, and then use them to make irresistible *Baconish* recipes from breakfast through dessert." —**Fran Costigan**, author of *Vegan Chocolate*

"The smart and inventive veggie-based bacons in *Baconish* bring so much spice, smoke, and sizzle that even your hipster, bacon-fetishist cousin will love them. Finally, vegans can safely, healthily, and deliciously take part in America's favorite pastime—putting bacon on, in, and around everything." —**Brian L. Patton**, author of *The Sexy Vegan Cookbook* and *The Sexy Vegan's Happy Hour at Home*

"As I paged through this book, the 'Hallelujah Chorus' started to play in my head, and my mouth began to water. It's a complete game changer for those who are resisting going plant-based out of a fear of missing bacon, and it's a must-have for any former bacon lovers who have gone veg. A revelatory work that will save many lives—human and porcine alike." —**Marisa Miller Wolfson**, writer and director of *Vegucated*

"I can't wait to make all these vegan bacons and let the yumminess waft into my hipster-filled Williamsburg neighborhood and then when they line up at my door, jump out covered in seitan and shiitake and say 'Ha! It's 0 percent pig, 100 percent delicious, bitches.'" —**Leanne Mai-ly Hilgart**, founder and president of Vaute Couture

"These recipes will expand your palate and your mind around what bacon is and, more importantly, what it can be. Chocolate-Peanut Bacon Truffles anyone? Yes, please! This book is post "real" bacon and is indeed the future of bacon. Be brave and step into the future!" —**Chef Ayindé Howell**, lifelong vegan and coauthor of *The Lusty Vegan*

"Leinana's book on vegan bacon is revelatory for animal lovers, vegans, and—perhaps most interestingly—us kosher folk who've never even tried bacon but curiously wonder what all the fuss is about! We will have a blast playing with these divine, smoky recipes that are cruelty-free and good for the bod, the animals, and Mother Earth." —**Chloé Jo Davis**, founder and editor of GirlieGirl Army

"Leinana has cracked the bacon code and now everyone on earth can enjoy smoky, savory goodness without the attached heartburn, cholesterol, or dead animals. Leinana for president!" —**Laura Beck**, founding editor of Vegansaurus.com

"There's something about the combination of salt, fat, and smoke that triggers a sacred pleasure center in the brain. It's a nostalgic, bold, and satisfying gastronomic triad. Leinana Two Moons is part alchemist, part hedonist in this crave-worthy collection of recipes that will expand anyone's vegetable vocabulary in the uncanny realm of the crisp and *umami.* Let anyone who thinks bacon only comes from pigs kneel at the altar of cured, complex, and succulent mushroom, coconut, eggplant, chickpea, seitan, and carrot bacon." —**Joshua Katcher**, founder of TheDiscerningBrute.com and BraveGentleMan.com

"In *Baconish,* Leinana Two Moons turns the bacon craze on its head, managing—in one heart-happy book—to both validate our nation's obsession with bacon while also offering mouthwatering recipes for anyone hungry for something better. Whether you sing the praises of animal-based bacon or you took animals off your plate long ago, this book will leave you pleasantly surprised by the palate-pleasing, plant-based alternatives. *Baconish* is nothing short of life-change-ish." —**Jasmin Singer**, author of *Always Too Much and Never Enough and* host of *Our Hen House* podcast

"Leinana was so passionate about vegan bacons before most of us even imagined, much less knew about, the many ways to make it. No surprise then that she can pull off a cookbook about vegan bacon that leaves one salivating for this beloved food. Thanks to her, we can get our bacon on while leaving pigs to live in peace!" —**Demetrius Bagley**, producer of *Vegucated* and *Vegan Mashup*

"I have known Leinana for many years and I am excited to try her new book! As an executive chef, I love the sweet, salty flavor of bacon, and I can't wait to dig into her recipes." —**Doug McNish**, vegan chef and author of *Vegan Everyday*

BACON·ISH

SULTRY AND SMOKY PLANT-BASED RECIPES
FROM BLTS TO BACON MAC & CHEESE

LEINANA
Two Moons

with a foreword by Annie Shannon

VEGAN HERITAGE PRESS
Woodstock • Virginia

ISBN: 978-1-941252-24-6

First Printing, April 2016

10 9 8 7 6 5 4 3 2 1

Vegan Heritage Press, LLC books are available at quantity discounts. For information, please visit our website at www.veganheritagepress.com or write the publisher at Vegan Heritage Press, P.O. Box 628, Woodstock, VA 22664-0628.

Library of Congress Cataloging-in-Publication Data
Names: Two Moons, Leinana, 1975- author.
Title: Baconish : sultry and smoky plant-based recipes from blts to bacon mac
  & cheese / by Leinana Two Moons.
Description: Woodstock, VA : Vegan Heritage Press, [2016] | Includes
  bibliographical references and index.
Identifiers: LCCN 2016001063| ISBN 9781941252246 (pbk. : alk. paper) | ISBN
  9781941252253 (e-book : alk. paper) | ISBN 9781941252260 (prc ebook : alk.
  paper)
Subjects: LCSH: Meat substitutes. | Bacon. | Vegan cooking. | LCGFT:
  Cookbooks.
Classification: LCC TX838 .T86 2016 | DDC 641.5/636--dc23 LC record available at http://lccn.loc.gov/2016001063

Photo credits: Photography and food styling by Anthony Two Moons and Leinana Two Moons. Front cover photo of Seitan Bacon (page 16). Back cover photos (left to right) Denver Omelet (page 64), Carrot Bacon (page 29), and Elvis Cupcakes (page 178).

Disclaimer: The information provided in this book should not be taken as medical advice. If you require a medical diagnosis or prescription, or if you are contemplating any major dietary change consult a qualified health-care provider. Neither the publisher nor the author are responsible for readers' health issues.

Publisher's Note: The information in this book is correct and complete to the best of our knowledge. The publisher is not responsible for specific health or allergy issues regarding ingredients used in this book.

Vegan Heritage Press books are distributed by Andrews McMeel Publishing.

Printed in the United States of America

Dedication

To my sous-chefs, Bodhi and Dahlia.

You make me want to make the world a better place for you.

And to the pigs.

I want to make the world a better place for you, too.

Contents

8. MAINS

9. SWEETS AND SUCH

Foreword

Bacon lovers. We've all met them. He's that friend from high school who posts recycled memes on Facebook declaring his devotion to BLTs—hold the L and T. She's the girl at the bar with a tee shirt telling us to "Keep Calm and Eat Bacon." They're the avid commenters on vegan blogs compelled to express their passion for this pork product in all CAPS and explain in long rambling posts how deeply they don't care how pig farms are unthinkably cruel and terrible for the environment, because bacon. Bacon. Bacon. *Bacon.*

It's a broken record heard on vegan blogs everywhere. Every time I see one of these comments I'm reminded of something another sort of Bacon once said. Sir Francis Bacon, that is:

"A wise man will make more opportunities than he finds."

See, this is where vegans ultimately win. With Baconish, we can now eat our "bacon" and not worry about our cholesterol. With a clear conscious, we can enjoy that signature smoky, savory flavor that can both accentuate the sweet maple glaze on a doughnut and add that bit of awesome that makes a bacon cheeseburger the icon it's become. Plant-based bacons have created a whole new cruelty-free arena for one of the culinary world's biggest food trends. Therein lies the genius of this book.

This isn't your mom's hippy granola cookbook from college. It isn't full of hummus wraps and lentil loaves. It tackles new novelties you never even knew you'd love, like ice cream sundaes sprinkled with vegan bacon bits, and shows you how to make bacons from scratch using your own coconut, seitan, tempeh, eggplant, mushrooms, and carrots. It's a book pigs all over the world have been waiting for, because it proves yet again that going vegan doesn't mean giving anything up—it just means you've found a more compassionate way to live.

It makes sense that a book with such clever and kind recipes would come from my friend Leinana Two Moons. We first met via Twitter back in 2009 after I started sharing recipes on a blog I started just for fun. She reached out to me out of nowhere to offer encouragement in 140 characters or less—a gesture that changed my life forever. After I moved to Brooklyn, she became more than just my friend: Leinana became one of my most trusted recipe testers (a beloved position in my world, not that different from the Sicilian consiglieri in *The Godfather).* Through more than five years, two books, and hundreds of recipes, Leinana has given it to me straight while still keeping an open mind and sense of humor. And I'm not the only one.

So many of the cookbooks we all use on a daily basis have benefited from her willingness to be the first to try out some new way to use chickpeas or quinoa. The impact Leinana has made on the world of vegan cookbooks is already significant. So it makes sense that her first book would not only completely redefine the idea that everything is better with bacon, but also do it in such a delicious and kind-hearted way.

—Annie Shannon, author of *Betty Goes Vegan*
and *Mastering the Art of Vegan Cooking*

Introduction

Learning to cook vegan food was somewhat born of necessity for me, having married a vegan man who does not cook (fortunately, he has other redeeming qualities). Actually, when we first married, I was not vegan, as I still ate seafood and dairy products. Out of convenience, I cooked only vegan food for us at home, so we could eat the same thing. We would go out on dates, though, and I would always end up with "food envy," preferring his vegan dishes to whatever I had ordered. Little by little, I started eliminating animal products altogether, and at some point I noticed health issues that I'd had my entire life were suddenly disappearing. Digestive problems and respiratory issues vanished, my allergies cleared up, and my skin stopped breaking out. I felt better than ever on a vegan diet—and then one evening, after watching the movie *Earthlings,* I stopped buying leather goods and other animal products, and declared myself vegan from that point on.

Inspired by vegan cookbook authors and bloggers, I began expanding my culinary repertoire with great enthusiasm. We began attending vegan events in the city and became part of a large and socially active vegan community in New York City. I began to document my cooking endeavors, vegan restaurant reviews, and events that we attended on my blog, *Vegan Good Things,* in an effort to share and connect with even more people.

Since the births of my two children, I am constantly being tested for inspiration, creativity, and resourcefulness. I'm now cooking and developing new recipes for a picky preschooler, a toddler, and a husband who suddenly declared himself gluten- and sugar-free.

Despite the challenges, I have two happy, healthy, and thriving vegan children whom I am trying to raise to be thoughtful, compassionate human beings. There is a natural compassion in children toward animals that becomes disconnected when we teach them that some animals are worthy of love and affection and others are simply destined to become our food.

Of course, I wasn't raised vegan. I was raised on a very typical, American, meat-and-potatoes type of diet. My father loves to remind me of how much I used to love a certain fast-food chain's junior bacon cheeseburgers. I'm sure he finds it ironic now that I'm vegan and writing a book about vegan bacon. It's been a long journey from junior bacon cheeseburgers to vegan bacon. I hope this book will interest everyone who loves bacon—and everyone who loves animals even more than they love bacon.

XO,

Leinana

Top to bottom: Seitan Bacon (page 16), Tempeh Bacon (page 19), and Tofu Bacon (page 18)

Happy Healthy Bacon

· ·

"I could never go vegan because of bacon."

I can't tell you how many times I've heard that line. I've even heard of a so-called vegetarian who made an "exception" for bacon. Well, I'm here to tell you that you can live without animal-based bacon. In fact, you'll most likely live longer without it.

But that doesn't mean that your taste buds have to suffer or that you have to deprive yourself of that smoky, savory, crispy deliciousness that is the essence of bacon. You can have your vegan bacon and eat it, too!

Everybody Loves the Flavors of Bacon

I'm going to let you in on a secret here: vegans love to eat delicious bacon, too. And you know what? Vegans can make bacon out of lots of ingredients. It's a fact. Just peruse a handful of vegan blogs and you will surely come across a number of homemade bacon recipes. Not because vegans miss eating pigs, but because there is something undeniably satisfying about the combination of salty, smoky, and crispy, which is what bacon is really all about.

This book introduces you to many of the delicious ways you can enjoy plant-based bacon, beginning with making your own from a variety of ingredients. The baconish recipes made with hearty ingredients such as tofu, tempeh, and seitan might remind you more of the traditional bacon, although if you haven't tried coconut bacon before, you're going to be amazed at how it mimics the crispy, fatty texture of traditional bacon. Because mushrooms are loaded with natural umami (savory flavor), it takes very little seasoning to transform them into tasty little baconish morsels. Your salads will get a lot more exciting with the addition of eggplant- and carrot-based bacons. And you can top all kinds of things with the Roasted Chickpea Bacon, from soups and salads to pasta and grains (or you can just snack on them right out of the bowl).

My intention is to celebrate the deliciousness and creativity that comes from making bacon out of plant-based ingredients. Vegan bacon is every bit as versatile as the pig version; you can use it in an infinite number of ways. The recipes in this collection were selected as most representative of the wide range of ways you can use vegan bacon and are meant to inspire your own creativity and ideas for other uses.

Things To Do with Vegan Bacon

As with any other type of bacon, you can enjoy vegan bacon in a number of delicious ways:

- Pile it high in your sandwiches, burgers, and wraps
- Toss it into your salads
- Sprinkle it on top of your soups
- Fold it into your vegan omelet
- Sprinkle it on your baked potato
- Mix it into your pasta
- Put some on your pizza

- Add it to your vegetables

- Cover it with chocolate

- Mix it into your homemade ice cream

- Eat it alongside your pancakes or waffles

- Put it *in* your pancakes or waffles

Or just munch it by the handful. The possibilities are endless.

These recipes are easy to make at home with ingredients that are generally easy to find in most grocery stores. While the recipes are animal-friendly, they were created to satisfy even the most hardcore bacon fiend. They are also versatile and meant to be used freely and interchangeably whenever the salty, smoky, crispy craving strikes. For each recipe, I recommend the types of bacon that I generally use for that particular dish, but feel free to experiment and use other types of vegan bacon to suit your own preferences.

I'm not trying to fool anyone with these recipes or claim that they taste exactly like bacon made from pigs. Obviously, some will taste more "meaty" than others, but all of them try to capture the smoky, sultry savoriness. I hope you discover and appreciate that plant-based bacon is delicious in its own right and is every bit as versatile as the "real" thing.

Sodium Alert

If you are concerned about sodium in your diet, I want to remind you that this is a cookbook about bacon. My recipes use salt, tamari or soy sauce, and plant-based fats in order to create as much bacon flavor as possible. You may want to try making the recipes using a lower-sodium tamari, for example, but doing so will scale back the salty element. To paraphrase the words of Cookie Monster, bacon is what we could call a "sometimes food." You aren't meant to eat it with every meal, every day, or the entire batch all in one sitting. But if you do, then just make sure you drink plenty of water. And maybe eat a green salad, because we can't live on bacon alone.

Top Ten Reasons to Eat Vegan Bacon

....

1. Vegan bacon is delicious! It's crispy, crunchy, smoky, and salty—everything you look for in bacon. Seriously, try some Coconut Bacon (page 21) right now. You'll thank me.

2. Bacon made from pigs is loaded with saturated fat and cholesterol, high levels of which lead to higher risks of heart disease and stroke. Vegan food is naturally cholesterol-free and far lower in fat.

3. Multiple studies show that processed meats like bacon and sausages are undeniably linked to heart attacks, strokes, and bowel and pancreatic cancers.

4. Pigs know their names, wag their tails when they're happy, and are capable of rescuing their human companions, just like dogs. In fact, pigs are proven to be smarter and more trainable than dogs. Did you know that pigs can put together puzzles and learn to play video games?

5. Coconut Bacon. Seriously.

6. Vegan bacon is so much more creative and versatile than animal bacon could ever be. I mean, there's eggplant bacon. Who was the first person to think of that? Vegans are such geniuses.

7. You can make things such as eggplant bacon, carrot bacon, or mushroom bacon, and get all the satisfying deliciousness of eating pig bacon, but you still get to tell yourself that you're eating a serving of vegetables. Win-win.

8. Pig bacon isn't just bad for your health. It's bad for the environment, too. Animal agriculture pollutes our water, it is the number one contributor of greenhouse gas emissions, and it requires exponentially more water to produce meat than to produce vegetables.

9. Do a Google Image search for "baby pigs." Just do it.

10. Did I mention Coconut Bacon?

How Baconish Came to Be

To understand how I came up with the idea for an all-vegan bacon cookbook, I'll tell you how this journey began. It all started way back in the summer of 2010.

My husband and I took a long-weekend trip to Montreal. We ate our way through all the best vegan spots in the city, but one of the highlights was a casual little vegan eatery named Aux Vivres. There, I was introduced to the magic that is coconut bacon. I had never heard of it before, but I was immediately intrigued, so I ordered the BLT and immediately fell in love with it. From the first bite, my mind was blown. It was crunchy, crispy, salty, and smoky—it felt like I was munching on actual bacon. It was uncanny. It was delicious. I begged our server to tell me how they made it, but with a sly grin he politely refused. From that moment on, I was obsessed with coconut bacon, and I made it a mission to re-create it as soon as I got home. Fortunately, there were many recipes floating around on the Internet, and when I made my own variation and posted it on my blog, *Vegan Good Things,* it immediately went viral. This sandwich is the most popular post on my blog. People just can't get enough coconut bacon! I have fine-tuned the recipe for this book, and you can find it on page 107.

After the coconut bacon craze, I began seeing recipes for all different types of vegan bacon pop up on the Internet. Mushroom bacon. Seitan bacon. Eggplant bacon. Carrot bacon. Vegan bacon was everywhere, and I thought it would be a great idea to put together one collection of lots of different ways to make vegan bacon, with recipes highlighting the many ways to cook with it and use it.

Why Not Animal-Based Bacon?

It shouldn't be a surprise that the coconut bacon caught on as much as it did, as it seems to be part of the overall bacon craze. I mean, unless you've been living in a cave for the last several years, you've probably noticed that bacon is kind of a thing. It's a thing that's not showing any signs of going away. In addition to the kind of bacon you eat, there is bacon-flavored lip gloss, bacon vodka, bacon lollipops, bacon-flavored toothpaste, bacon-flavored soda, bacon-flavored dental floss, bacon-flavored . . . well, you get my drift.

Indeed, the bacon craze continues despite overwhelming evidence that eating it is terrible for you. Bacon made from pigs is loaded with saturated fat and cholesterol, high levels of which lead to higher risks of heart disease and stroke. Most bacon is also loaded with nitrates, which are used as preservatives, and which have been linked in multiple studies to higher risks of heart disease and cancer. A Harvard University study found that *just one serving* of bacon or other processed meat per day led to a significant increase in death from cancer and heart disease. Processed meats like bacon and sausage are undeniably linked to heart attacks, strokes, and bowel and pancreatic cancers.

If that's not enough to convince you that eating animal-based bacon is a serious risk to your health, then perhaps the findings of the World Health Organization will. In October 2015, while I was still completing this book, WHO's International Agency for Research on Cancer concluded that eating processed meats (including bacon, ham, sausages, hot dogs, canned meats, and so on) causes colorectal cancer. Not "probably" causes colorectal cancer. It causes it. Full stop.

Their report was prepared by twenty-two public health and cancer experts from ten different countries and was based on the review of eight hundred studies on cancer in humans. The report stated that 50 grams of processed meat per day (which is less than two slices of bacon) increases the risk of colorectal cancer by 18 percent. Why processed meat causes cancer is still unclear. The link between processed meats and cancer may be due to an iron-based chemical in meat called heme, which breaks down into carcinogenic compounds in the digestive tract; or it might be due to the nitrates and nitrites used to preserve these meats; or it may be due to the carcinogenic compounds created by cooking meat at high temperatures (grilling, frying, or pan-frying). Or it could be any combination of those factors.

WHO's findings place bacon and other processed meats squarely into the known carcinogenic "Group 1" category, among other known cancer-causing agents, including plutonium, asbestos, alcohol, tobacco, and air pollution. Granted, they are not saying that eating bacon has as severe and immediate risk for cancer as say, exposure to plutonium, but whether it leads to cancer quickly or slowly is not really a debate that I find worth discussing. Why risk it at all when there are so many other delicious things to eat? When there are plenty of ways to satisfy those baconish cravings without sacrificing your health?

Even More Reasons to Love Pigs, Not Eat Them

But pig bacon isn't just bad for your health. It's bad news for our planet, too. Agricultural runoff is the number one cause of pollution in our waterways. Livestock farming accounts for more than half of all worldwide greenhouse gas emissions. Animal agriculture consumes more than half of the total amount of water in the United States. Two-thirds of all agricultural land in the United States is used to raise animals for food and to grow grain to feed these animals destined for slaughter. How many more people could we feed and how many resources could we save if we grew grains and other plants for people to eat instead?

And lest we forget, how bad is the bacon craze for the pigs themselves? Pigs are smart. They know their names and wag their tails when they're happy, just like dogs. In fact,

pigs are proven to be smarter and more trainable than dogs. They are even smarter than the average three-year-old child. I have a three-year-old son, and let me tell you, he's pretty smart. But pigs are one of the most intelligent animals, closely behind apes and dolphins. They love attention, to be touched and massaged, and they are loyal, gentle, sensitive, and affectionate beings. They form friendships, greet each other, and sleep snuggled up or nose-to-nose. They are individuals with their own unique personalities. Like all animals, they have a will to live and their lives are not ours to take.

You may have heard of Esther the Wonder Pig, who was adopted by a Canadian couple. When they adopted Esther, they were told that she was a miniature pig who wouldn't grow to be more than 70 pounds. To their great surprise, she was actually a typical farm pig, who has grown to over 600 pounds. By the time they realized that they had been duped, they had bonded with Esther, and she had grown used to a comfortable home life. They had already come to know her unique personality, so instead of giving her up, the whole family moved to a larger home where Esther could live and have outdoor space. You can follow Esther's escapades on social media or via their website, http://www.estherthewonderpig. com/. Indeed, Esther seems to be a wonderful pig, but the only difference between her and other pigs is that she was allowed to live and let her personality be known. Perhaps if pigs didn't grow up to be such large animals, many more of them would share our homes as companion animals instead of winding up on dinner plates.

There's No Better Time to Be Vegan

Being vegan is easier than ever. There is a wealth of options in every grocery store that simply did not exist even a few years ago. There are plant-based meat alternatives and vegan milks that taste far better than the animal-based versions. There has been a recent explosion of incredible new vegan cheeses that would make even the French proud. And there is an amazing online community of vegan bloggers who are always inspiring and stunning with their creativity, resourcefulness, and culinary mastery, making and sharing recipes for dishes we thought would be impossible to veganize. (Just check out the Facebook group for Vegan Meringues—Hits and Misses if you want to be amazed at what vegan home cooks can do!)

Being vegan is certainly not about deprivation. The vegans I know are some of the most food-loving—dare I say, food-worshipping—people I have ever known. We eat abundantly, we eat decadently. We eat fun, interesting, flavorful, and delicious food. And we never feel guilty about it.

Ingredients You'll Need

I've tried my best to use ingredients that are generally easy to find in most grocery stores or health food stores. Nevertheless, there may be some ingredients that are less familiar to you, if you are new to vegan cooking, so I've described them for you here.

Agar powder – Derived from algae, agar is a vegan alternative to gelatin, which is made from animal by-products. Agar is sold in small flakes or in powder form and can be used to make jellies, custards, or puddings. It is generally found in health food stores.

Apple cider vinegar (ACV) – I usually buy Bragg brand apple cider vinegar, which is organic, raw, and unfiltered. Made from organic apples, it lends a freshness and brightness to many recipes. There are a lot of health benefits to ACV, from aiding digestion to soothing irritated skin or a sore throat.

Aquafaba – What is aquafaba? Aquafaba is simply the liquid that you pour out of a can of chickpeas or other beans. (The term, coined by blogger Goose Wohlt, comes from the Latin *aqua* [water] and *faba* [bean].) The liquid, which people normally wash down the drain, is actually rich in protein from the beans, and it magically whips up into a meringue, just like egg whites. It can also be used on its own as a general egg replacer in most recipes when an egg would normally be called for as a binder. I use aquafaba quite often and find that it makes baked goods incredibly moist. If you are wondering what to do with the leftover chickpeas, make Roasted Chickpea Bacon! (**Note:** As an egg replacer, 3 tablespoons of aquafaba is equal to one egg.)

Black salt – I use this sparingly in some of the "egg" recipes. This salt is high in sulfuric content, which gives it an unmistakable eggy odor. When you use it, you only need a small pinch. This is potent stuff.

Chickpeas – Also known as garbanzos, these small, round legumes are very high in protein, fiber, folate, and a bunch of other good stuff. They can be cooked and eaten whole, pureed into a spread (like hummus), or ground into flour (see below). They are also delicious when roasted and made into chickpea bacon.

Chickpea flour – Also known as gram flour or besan, this is used often in Indian cuisine. For vegan dishes, it is mixed with water or other liquids for use as an egg replacer.

Jackfruit – This fruit is native to southern Asia and has recently experienced a surge in popularity as a meat replacer in savory recipes. When the fruit is shredded, its texture has an uncanny resemblance to shredded meat, such as pulled pork. If you are using it in a savory recipe, be sure to use the type that is canned in brine or water, not syrup.

Kelp granules – This is a type of dried seaweed. It is rich in iodine and nutrients from the sea, and it is often used as a low-sodium salt alternative. It can be used as a seasoning in many types of recipes.

Kimchi – This spicy, fermented Korean cabbage dish is sometimes made with cucumbers, radishes, or other vegetables. Think of it as a hot and spicy Asian version of sauerkraut. Fermented foods have great health benefits, like introducing probiotics (beneficial bacteria) into your system and aiding digestion. Kimchi can be found in any Korean market (or most other Asian grocery stores) and health food stores, or you can make your own using the recipe on page 117. I am somewhat addicted to this stuff, which is probably why it shows up in so many of my recipes.

Large-flake coconut – You'll need this to make coconut bacon. It is the large, white, untoasted flakes, not sweetened or shredded.

Liquid smoke – I rely on liquid smoke to provide the smokiness of my vegan bacon. Liquid smoke is quite simply condensed smoke mixed with water. It is very concentrated, and you need only use small amounts for a lot of aroma and flavor.

Maple syrup – Most of my bacon recipes call for maple syrup to add a touch of sweetness, as well as its maple flavor that goes so well with bacon. We use pure maple syrup with no added sugar.

Miso paste – The fermented soybean paste, which is the basis of the familiar miso soup, is salty and rich in umami (or savory flavor). Miso paste comes in many varieties. In general, the darker the color, the richer and deeper the flavor. It can be used in soups, sauces, dressings, and many other dishes to add an extra savoriness and depth of flavor.

Store-Bought Ingredients

As a busy mother of two, I tend to buy a few other ready-made ingredients in order to save time, rather than making my own. Store-bought ingredients that I use in my recipes include marinara sauce for pasta and barbecue sauce. Feel free to buy ready-to-use pizza dough, biscuit dough, pie crusts, and other ingredients if you don't have time to make them from scratch.

Nutritional yeast – Lovingly referred to as "nooch" by many vegans, nutritional yeast is a lot tastier than it sounds. It is an excellent source of vitamin B_{12}, the only vitamin that is missing from plant-based foods. It is used in a vast number of vegan recipes for its "cheesy" and savory qualities, and it's often used in vegan "egg" dishes both to add color and flavor. You can use it in pretty much everything, from sprinkling it on popcorn to using it as the base for a vegan macaroni and cheese sauce.

Smoked paprika – Smoked paprika is created by drying chiles over a wood fire to infuse them with a smoky, woodsy flavor, and then grinding them into powder. It is generally not very hot but has a deep flavor and helps add smoky notes to our vegan bacon recipes.

Smoked salt – If you think that smoked salt is a new and trendy thing, apparently the Vikings were way ahead of us—they were known to infuse their salt with smoke from wood fires. Many different types of wood can be used, such as alder, apple, hickory, mesquite, and oak, each of which gives the salt a slightly different flavor.

Smoked tofu – This is tofu that has been smoked, often in tea leaves, or alternatively made by simply adding liquid smoke. I love smoked tofu for its savory flavor and for its firm texture—it can be eaten straight out of the package and doesn't need any pressing. It is the base for my tofu bacon recipe.

Sriracha sauce – This spicy Thai condiment seems to be ubiquitous these days. It is an outrageously addictive sauce made from chiles, vinegar, garlic, sugar, and salt. Fun fact: my family is actually from the Si Racha region of Thailand, where this condiment originated. So, basically, I have Sriracha sauce running through my veins.

Tahini – Made from ground sesame seeds, this sauce has a rich, nutty flavor and can be used in dressings, sauces, and many other types of recipes.

Tamari – This is what we rely on the most to provide the saltiness of our vegan bacon, as well as providing the umami (savory flavor) found in roasted meats. Tamari is similar to soy sauce and both are made from fermented soybeans. I generally prefer tamari in my cooking, because I find that it has a deeper, more balanced flavor than the straight saltiness of soy sauce. However, we're making bacon here, and salt is what we want, so feel free to use either one interchangeably. Soy sauce does contain wheat, so if you're avoiding gluten, you'll want to use a gluten-free tamari.

Tempeh – Originating in Indonesia, tempeh is made by cooking and fermenting soybeans then forming them into a firm "cake." The fermentation process makes tempeh more nutritious and digestible than other soy products. It has a slightly nutty and bitter flavor on its own, but readily absorbs marinades. It holds together well when sliced and is highly popular as a type of vegan bacon.

Textured vegetable protein (TVP) – Textured vegetable protein is a by-product of extracting soybean oil from soy flour. It is protein-rich, requires rehydration before use, and is often used as an analogue to ground meat in recipes. It is relatively inexpensive and easy to use.

Tofu – Tofu's reputation has come a long way from being thought of as "hippie health food" to now being well respected and showing up on the menus of even the finest restaurants. It comes in many forms, which can be used for different types of recipes.

- **Silken tofu** has the smoothest texture and is very soft and delicate. It is best used in recipes where it will be blended up, like sauces, smoothies, or egg substitutions.

- **Soft tofu** has more texture than silken, but like silken it is quite soft and has a high water content. It is great to use in desserts and as a substitute for eggs.

- **Extra-firm tofu** is what I use most in cooking savory dishes. It is more compact and denser than the other kinds of tofu, and holds up well to being baked, fried, or stir-fried. For most recipes using extra-firm tofu, I highly recommend pressing it first. Pressing will squeeze out the excess water, which will allow the tofu to absorb more marinade, brown faster and more evenly, and have a better texture. There are handy tofu presses you can order, or you can do it yourself by simply placing the block of tofu between clean dish towels or paper towels. Put a plate or other flat surface on top, and weigh it down with heavy items, like books or canned goods. Twenty to thirty minutes is usually sufficient to press out most of the water.

- **Super-firm tofu** is the densest, and as you might guess, the firmest of the bunch. I like to use it because it doesn't require pressing before being cooked. It can be harder to find, however, and is slightly more expensive.

Turmeric – This bright yellow, pungent spice is used widely in Indian curries and mustard blends. It is reputed to have a wealth of medicinal properties, including aiding indigestion, relieving joint pain and arthritis, preventing heart attacks, and more. I use it in a lot of the vegan "egg" dishes both for its earthy flavor and for the color.

Vegan cheese – Vegan cheese has come a long way. There has been a serious boom recently in vegan cheese brands, and it is now easier than ever to find vegan versions of everything from French Brie to Havarti. Many vegan cheeses are made from nut milks, especially cashew, while the popular brand Daiya uses tapioca as its base, and Field Roast Chao Slices are made from coconut oil and fermented tofu (which tastes a whole lot better than it sounds). For the recipes in this book, I recommend Daiya shreds and slices or Field Roast Chao Slices for their flavor and because they seem to be the most widely available in grocery and health food stores.

Vital wheat gluten – Vital wheat gluten is the natural protein found in wheat. It is what gives dough its elastic quality and is made by washing wheat flour until all the starches are dissolved, leaving only the stretchy, gummy gluten behind. It has been widely used in Asia since the sixth century as an alternative to meat. It is used to make seitan.

Worcestershire sauce – Traditional brands of Worcestershire sauce contain anchovies, so I recommend Annie's Naturals Organic Vegan Worcestershire Sauce. It adds a tangy, flavorful complexity to many different types of dishes.

Equipment You'll Use

For these recipes, I have tried to simplify the equipment as much as possible. With the exception of specialty equipment like doughnut pans to make the Maple-Bacon Doughnuts (page 68), most of the bacon recipes require little more than:

Baking sheets – For most recipes, I either use 11 x 17-inch or 10 x 15-inch rimmed baking sheets.

Cooling and baking racks – Use these to fit in the baking sheets.

Parchment paper or aluminum foil – These are useful to line the baking sheets.

Blender – A high-speed blender like a Vitamix is best for making the smoothest sauces and fillings, like the cashew-based filling I use in my vegan quiches. A regular blender will also work just fine.

Food processor – A food processor can be used to quickly chop and puree ingredients. It can also substitute for a high-speed blender, although, depending on the model you have, it may not get mixtures as smooth as a blender can.

Nonstick skillet – Some items are best cooked in a nonstick skillet. I will specify when this is the best option.

Cast iron skillet – I find that cast iron skillets are best when you want to get a nice caramelization on certain items. I will specify when this is the best option.

Vegan Egg Replacers

Each of the following is equivalent to one egg. Keep in mind that ingredients like banana or applesauce may change the flavor of your dish, so they are best used in baking, where the flavors will be complementary:

- 1 tablespoon ground flax seeds + 3 tablespoons water
- 1/4 cup pureed silken tofu
- 1/2 large banana, mashed
- 2 teaspoons baking powder + 1 tablespoon vegetable oil + 2 tablespoons water
- 1/4 cup applesauce
- 1/4 cup vegan yogurt
- 3 tablespoons chickpea liquid (aquafaba)

Commercial egg replacers:

- Ener-G Egg Replacer (made from potato starch and tapioca starch): 1 1/2 teaspoons mix + 2 tablespoons warm water
- Bob's Red Mill Egg Replacer: 1 tablespoon mix + 3 tablespoons water
- Follow Your Heart VeganEgg: 2 tablespoons mix + 1/2 cup ice-cold water (This item is a total game changer, as it can be used in cooking and baking or scrambled or made into omelets, just like regular eggs!)

Seitan Bacon (page 16)

Meet the Bacons

. . . .

Salty. Smoky. Crispy. Savory. Different ingredients, different techniques. All meant to satisfy those baconish cravings, while still making you feel good about yourself. Prepare to be amazed at how humble ingredients like tofu, carrots, and even chickpeas can completely transform themselves into sultry, savory, crave-worthy snacks. You'll never look at a coconut the same after you experience coconut bacon. Eggplants and mushrooms, tempeh and seitan, they all get the baconish makeover here. And if that's not enough, I've added some bonus recipes at the end of this chapter for Sweet and Spicy Barbecue Jackfruit (page 35), Saucy Spicy Chorizo (page 36), Pineapple-Glazed Seitan Ham (page 38), and Pigs in a Blanket (page 40)—all of which are 100 percent pig-friendly and unbelievably delicious.

Seitan Bacon

Makes about 1 1/4 pounds (about 40 strips)

Making seitan for the first time can be intimidating, until you do it and realize how easy it can be. This seitan is so savory and delicious, it will satisfy any cravings for smoky, meaty, baconish flavor.

Dry ingredients:

2 cups vital wheat gluten
1/4 cup nutritional yeast
1 teaspoon smoked salt
1 teaspoon smoked paprika
1/2 teaspoon onion powder
1/2 teaspoon garlic powder

Wet ingredients:

1/2 cup vegetable broth
1/4 cup safflower or other neutral-tasting vegetable oil
1/4 cup tamari
1/4 cup maple syrup
2 tablespoons liquid smoke
2 tablespoons ketchup

Glaze:

1 tablespoon maple syrup
1 1/2 teaspoons liquid smoke
1 1/2 teaspoons coarsely ground black pepper
1 teaspoon smoked salt
1 tablespoon olive oil, for cooking

Preheat the oven to 350°F. Line a 9 x 5-inch loaf pan with aluminum foil, ensuring that the bottom is fully covered, and lightly spray the foil with nonstick cooking spray.

In a large bowl, combine the vital wheat gluten, nutritional yeast, smoked salt, smoked paprika, onion powder, and garlic powder and mix well. In a separate bowl, whisk together the vegetable broth, safflower oil, tamari, maple syrup, liquid smoke, and ketchup. Pour the wet ingredients into the dry ingredients, and stir until they are combined. Use your hands to knead the dough until it is smooth and uniform. Shape it into a small loaf, approximately 7 x 4 x 2 inches. Place the seitan loaf into the prepared pan.

In a medium bowl, whisk together the maple syrup, liquid smoke, pepper, and smoked salt. Pour the glaze over the seitan loaf, and use your hands if necessary to rub the pepper into the top of the loaf, so it sticks to the surface. Carefully seal the foil all around the loaf, ensuring that there are no areas where the glaze will leak. Otherwise, it will quickly smoke and burn, ruining your pan.

Bake the seitan for 40 minutes, then remove it from oven and let it cool enough to handle. Carefully cut the loaf into 1/8-inch slices.

Heat the olive oil in a large skillet over medium heat. Add the seitan slices and cook on both sides until crisped around the edges, about 2 minutes per side. Be careful, because the sugar in the glaze will caramelize and cause the slices to burn quickly.

Tofu Bacon (page 18)   Tempeh Bacon (page 19)   Seitan Bacon (opposite)

Tofu Bacon

Makes about 2 cups

There is something so satisfying to me about creating a bacon recipe made with tofu. In this recipe, humble tofu transforms into a salty, smoky treat that is crispy on the edges, yet still tender and chewy in the middle. This bacon is utterly addictive and you will find yourself absentmindedly snacking on slice after slice.

1 (8-ounce) package smoked tofu
1/4 cup tamari
2 tablespoons maple syrup
1 tablespoon tomato paste
1 tablespoon liquid smoke
1 teaspoon apple cider vinegar
1/2 teaspoon coarsely ground black pepper
1/4 teaspoon onion powder
1/4 teaspoon garlic powder
1 tablespoon olive or safflower oil (if pan-frying)
Nonstick cooking spray (if baking)

Use a sharp knife to cut the tofu into 1/8-inch strips.

Whisk the tamari, maple syrup, tomato paste, liquid smoke, apple cider vinegar, pepper, onion powder, and garlic powder together in a medium bowl. Place the tofu slices in a large shallow 9- x 13-inch baking dish or a gallon-size plastic freezer bag, then pour the marinade over the top. Make sure all the slices are evenly coated. Allow the tofu to marinate a minimum of 1 hour (several hours is even better; the longer it marinates, the more flavor it will have).

To pan-fry the Tofu Bacon (which is the cooking method I recommend), heat the oil in a large cast iron skillet over medium-high heat. I highly recommend using a cast iron skillet because the bacon slices will get more caramelization and crispier edges than they will in a nonstick skillet. Working in batches, place the bacon slices in a single layer in the oil and pan-fry until they are dark brown in spots and crispy around the edges. Using tongs or a spatula, flip the slices and fry until they are crisped and browned on the other side.

To bake the Tofu Bacon, preheat the oven to 400°F. Lightly spray two cooling racks and place them on top of two baking sheets lined with parchment paper. Arrange the bacon slices in single layers over the cooling racks. Bake for 15 to 20 minutes, keeping a close eye on the tofu during the last 5 minutes. The thinner the slices are, the faster they will begin to burn. Baking them in the oven will create a firmer, crunchier bacon and will omit the oil.

To make Lardons: Chop the cooked Tofu Bacon slices into 1/4-inch pieces. These are great to use in recipes like Brussels Sprouts with Bacon and Shallots (page 129), French Lentil Salad with Tofu Bacon Lardons (page 102), or Pasta Carbonara (page 142).

Tempeh Bacon
Makes about 18 strips

. . . .

In the vegan world, tempeh bacon recipes are nearly as ubiquitous as recipes for shepherd's pie. This one is my own personal version. It is salty, smoky, tender, and savory. I recommend marinating it overnight if you can. The longer you marinate the tempeh, the more flavorful it will be.

8 ounces soy tempeh
1/4 cup tamari
2 tablespoons maple syrup
1 tablespoon apple cider vinegar
1 tablespoon liquid smoke
2 tablespoons olive oil, divided
2 teaspoons tomato paste
1/2 teaspoon garlic powder

Using a long, serrated bread knife and cutting slightly at an angle, slice the tempeh lengthwise into approximately 18 (1/8-inch) strips.

In a medium bowl, whisk together the tamari, maple syrup, apple cider vinegar, liquid smoke, 1 tablespoon of the oil, tomato paste, and garlic powder.

Combine the tempeh and marinade in a large zip-top plastic bag or a shallow dish with a lid. Make sure the tempeh is evenly coated with the marinade. Marinate for several hours or, ideally, overnight.

To cook, heat the remaining 1 tablespoon of oil in a large skillet over medium-high heat. Add the tempeh strips, brushing with leftover marinade if desired, and cook for 2 to 3 minutes on each side until they are dark brown and crispy on the edges. Keep a close eye on the bacon and do not allow it to burn, as charred pieces can be very bitter.

Coconut Bacon

Makes 2 1/2 cups

When I posted this recipe on my blog, *Vegan Good Things,* back in 2010, people went crazy for it. To this day, it is by far the most popular and most searched-for post on the site. I've updated and fine-tuned it just a little bit, to get perfect results every time. This recipe will make any vegan-bacon skeptic a true believer. It is my absolute favorite bacon to use for the best BLTs ever.

3 tablespoons tamari
1 tablespoon liquid smoke
1 tablespoon water
1 tablespoon maple syrup
3 cups unsweetened large-flake coconut

Preheat the oven to 350°F. Whisk the tamari, liquid smoke, water, and maple syrup together in a large bowl. Stir in the coconut and mix well to ensure that the flakes are evenly coated.

Spread the coconut in an even layer on a large baking sheet lined with parchment paper. Bake 10 minutes, then stir. Bake another 8 minutes, keeping a very close eye on the coconut in the last few minutes. The coconut will go from almost done to completely burned very quickly. Remove from the oven when the coconut flakes on the outer edges of the pan are becoming a deep, dark brown, but not black.

Place the baking sheet on a cooling rack. The coconut will continue to crisp as it cools. Coconut bacon will keep 1 to 2 weeks in an airtight plastic container, but will become less crisp the longer you store it. So make those BLTs right now and eat up.

Eggplant Bacon
Makes about 1 1/2 cups

This recipe takes a bit longer than the others, but salting the eggplant will remove the bitterness and allow it to absorb more of the marinade. This bacon has just a hint of spice and is great to add to salads. I use regular Italian eggplants for this, because they are easier to find than the longer Asian variety (although if you have those, feel free to experiment with them, keeping in mind that smaller pieces will cook much faster).

1 medium Italian eggplant (about 1 pound)
1 1/2 teaspoons salt
1/4 cup tamari
1/2 teaspoon apple cider vinegar
1 tablespoon olive oil
1 tablespoon maple syrup
1/2 teaspoon smoked paprika
1/2 teaspoon ground cumin
1/2 teaspoon garlic powder
Ground black pepper, to taste

Trim the top and bottom off the eggplant. Peel the rest of the skin off with a vegetable peeler. Cut the eggplant in half lengthwise, then cut it crosswise into 1/4-inch thick half-moons.

Layer the eggplant slices in a colander that is placed in the sink or over a bowl. Sprinkle the salt on each layer, so that the slices are evenly coated. Set aside for a minimum of 20 to 30 minutes, then squeeze out the excess moisture and pat the slices dry with a paper towel or clean dishcloth.

Whisk together the tamari, apple cider vinegar, oil, maple syrup, smoked paprika, cumin, garlic powder, and several twists of black pepper in a large bowl. Add the eggplant slices and toss to coat evenly. Let the slices marinate at least 1 hour, tossing occasionally to ensure that the slices get evenly coated.

Preheat the oven to 250°F. Place a cooling rack (or two, depending on size) on top of a baking sheet lined with parchment paper. Lightly spray the rack with nonstick cooking spray, then place the eggplant slices in a single layer on the rack. Bake for 1 hour and 15 minutes. Let the eggplant bacon cool completely (it will continue to crisp as it cools), then store it in an airtight plastic container.

King Trumpet Mushroom Bacon
Makes about 1 cup

I love the hearty texture of king trumpet mushrooms—they have a lot more stem than cap, so they are a bit sturdier and less delicate than other varieties. (Keep in mind that mushrooms shrink dramatically when they are cooked!) This bacon is especially great sprinkled on stir-fries, fried rice, Asian greens, and salads.

- 1 tablespoon sesame oil
- 1 tablespoon tamari
- 1 teaspoon smoked paprika
- 8 ounces king trumpet mushrooms, lightly rinsed, patted dry, and cut lengthwise into 1/4-inch slices
- 1 teaspoon smoked salt

Preheat the oven to 375°F. Place a cooling rack on a large baking sheet lined with parchment paper. Lightly spray the rack with nonstick cooking spray.

In a medium bowl, whisk together the oil, tamari, and smoked paprika. Add the mushrooms and toss to coat. Sprinkle the mushrooms with the smoked salt and use your hands to toss again, until the mushrooms are evenly coated. They will be barely moistened, not wet.

Arrange the mushroom slices in a single layer on the cooling rack. It's okay if some slices overlap slightly. Bake for 25 to 28 minutes, keeping a close eye during the last few minutes so that they don't burn. You want the bacon to be a deep brown and crisped around the edges, but still pliant in the middle.

This bacon is best eaten right away, as it doesn't stay crisp when stored. If you must store some leftovers, I recommend lightly heating them in the oven to re-crisp.

Shiitake Mushroom Bacon
Makes about 1 cup

I love this super simple mushroom bacon. Mushrooms have so much satisfying natural umami flavor to them, they really don't need much seasoning. These get really nice and crispy and are perfect for sprinkling on top of soups, salads, rice dishes, or pretty much anything.

8 ounces shiitake mushrooms, lightly rinsed, patted dry, stems trimmed, and cut into 1/4-inch thick slices
1 tablespoon olive oil
1 tablespoon tamari
1 teaspoon smoked salt

Preheat the oven to 375°F. Line a large rimmed baking sheet with parchment paper.

Place the shiitakes in a medium bowl, then drizzle with the oil and tamari. Sprinkle with the smoked salt, and then use your hands to toss and make sure the shiitakes are evenly coated. They will be barely moistened, not wet.

Arrange the mushrooms in an even layer on the baking sheet. Bake for 30 minutes, stirring occasionally, and keeping a close eye toward the end to make sure they don't burn. These will store a few days in an airtight container but are best eaten immediately for maximum crispiness.

Seaweed Bacon?!

That's right! The red, leafy seaweed called dulse (rhymes with "pulse") tastes remarkably like smoky, savory bacon when pan-fried. Like all edible seaweeds, this superfood is incredibly nutrient-dense (with twice the nutritional value of kale), high in iodine, and even packs a major protein punch. Researchers at Oregon State University are developing ways to grow a newly patented dulse strain inexpensively and sustainably, to use in commercial food products featuring this baconish gift from the sea. Expect to see dulse featured in products like rice crackers, salad dressing, popcorn, and more in the near future. DLT sandwich, anyone?

Bacon Best Uses

Vegan bacon is incredibly versatile and can be used in as many different ways as pig-based bacon. Here's a guide for which vegan bacons to use in which types of dishes.

Tofu Bacon (page 18) absorbs marinade well and has a good firm texture. It makes an especially good replacement for recipes that call for ham or Canadian bacon and works best in sandwiches, salads, pasta, pizza, or any savory dish.

Tempeh Bacon (page 19) has a meaty texture and works well in any recipe using bacon. It holds up well in cooked dishes without losing its flavor. Long tempeh strips are flexible and ideal for wrapping around other ingredients, like vegan hot dogs, asparagus bundles, or mushroom scallops. It's great in sandwiches, salads, pasta, and bacon-wrapped recipes.

Seitan Bacon (page 16) is probably the closest to pig-based bacon in appearance and texture. Whether you use whole strips or chop it up into bits, it will work well in any kind of savory dish. Seitan Bacon works best for sandwiches, salads, pasta, or any savory dish.

Coconut Bacon (page 21) is deliciously crispy and adds a great texture to dishes. It is best used in recipes without a lot of liquid, so that it doesn't lose its crispiness. It is delicious in both savory and sweet recipes and works best in salads, sandwiches, or desserts.

Eggplant Bacon (page 22) works great in savory dishes without a lot of liquid, so that it doesn't lose its seasoning or crispiness. Eggplant Bacon works best for salads, sandwiches, and as a topping for pasta or pizza.

King Trumpet Mushroom Bacon (page 25) slices have a firm bite and a savory umami flavor that is great in salads, sandwiches, vegetable dishes, and Asian dishes.

Shiitake Mushroom Bacon (page 26) pieces make a crispy topping for soups, pastas, and casseroles. It's also good in salads, sandwiches, and Asian recipes.

Carrot Bacon (page 29) has a slight natural sweetness and adds a nice pop of color to your dish. It works best for salads and sandwiches and as a topping for pasta or vegetables.

Roasted Chickpea Bacon (page 30) is addictive, but these cruncy morsels don't stay crunchy for long so they are best eaten right away. They are ideal as a topping for salads or soups or as a snack.

Baconish Bits (page 32) are perfect any time you want extra crunchy, smoky, baconish flavor. They hold their crunch and flavor well in many types of dishes and work best for salads, soups, pasta, and sweets.

Carrot Bacon

Makes about 2 cups

So carrot bacon is a crazy thing that I first heard of from my friend Annie Shannon, author of *Betty Goes Vegan.* It just seemed to prove that vegans really can and will turn anything into bacon. Carrots don't really absorb a marinade like the other options here, so it's more about getting them sliced thinly and evenly so they get nice and crispy and adding some smoke and spice for flavor.

2 large carrots (the wider the better), scrubbed and patted dry
2 tablespoons olive oil
1 tablespoon maple syrup
1/2 teaspoon smoked paprika
1 teaspoon smoked salt
Ground black pepper, to taste

Preheat the oven to 425°F and line a large rimmed baking sheet with parchment paper.

Cut the carrots into 2- to 3-inch pieces. Place the carrots horizontally into the feed tube of your food processor, and use the slicing disk to create thin, even slices. Arranging them in the tube horizontally will ensure longer slices of the carrot pieces instead of the "coins" you will get if you feed the carrots in vertically.

Arrange the carrot slices in a single layer on the prepared baking sheet. Drizzle the carrots evenly with oil and maple syrup, and then sprinkle them evenly with smoked paprika, smoked salt, and pepper.

Bake the carrots for 18 to 22 minutes, until brown and crisp. Keep a close eye the last few minutes so that they don't burn. If the pieces around the edge of the sheet start to burn, stir them so that they finish cooking more evenly. This bacon is best eaten right away, as it doesn't stay very crisp when stored. If you must store some leftovers, I recommend lightly heating them in the oven to re-crisp.

Roasted Chickpea Bacon

Makes 1 1/4 cups

....

Move over, hummus! There's a much more glamorous chickpea dish in town. Here, the humble chickpea shows the world how it can transform into a smoky, salty, crunchy, utterly addictive delight, with just a hint of sweetness from brown sugar. These are perfect for topping salads, soups, adding to sandwich wraps, or just munching straight from the bowl. In fact, you might find yourself making double batches just to keep plenty of these snacks on hand.

  1 (15-ounce) can chickpeas, drained and rinsed
  1 tablespoon plus 1 teaspoon olive oil, divided
  2 tablespoons tamari
  1 teaspoon liquid smoke
  1 teaspoon brown sugar
  1/4 teaspoon smoked salt

Preheat the oven to 425°F. Line a small baking sheet with parchment paper. Using paper towels or a clean dishcloth, pat the chickpeas as dry as possible. The drier they are, the crunchier they will get. If there are any loose skins, pick those out and discard them.

In a medium bowl, whisk together 1 tablespoon of the oil, tamari, and liquid smoke. Add the chickpeas and toss until they are evenly coated.

Transfer the chickpeas to the baking sheet and arrange them in a single layer. Bake for 20 minutes, take them out to stir, and then bake another 10 minutes or until the chickpeas are dark brown and crunchy.

In another medium bowl, combine the remaining 1 teaspoon oil, brown sugar, and smoked salt. Add the warm chickpeas and toss until evenly coated. Serve warm or at room temperature. These will last a couple of days in an airtight container stored at room temperature but will lose their crunch, so it's best to eat these immediately.

Baconish Bits

Makes about 1 cup

It's fairly easy to find accidentally vegan bacon bits at the grocery store, but they may contain preservatives and other questionable ingredients. These bits are easy to make yourself, healthier, and taste so much better than the store-bought kind.

1/4 cup boiling water
2 tablespoons tamari
1 tablespoon maple syrup
1 tablespoon liquid smoke
1 teaspoon ketchup
1/2 teaspoon garlic powder
1/2 teaspoon onion powder
1 cup texturized vegetable protein (TVP) (page 11)
2 tablespoons safflower or other neutral-tasting vegetable oil

In a medium bowl, whisk together the boiling water, tamari, maple syrup, liquid smoke, ketchup, garlic powder, and onion powder. Mix in the TVP and stir until it is evenly coated.

Heat the oil in a large skillet (preferably cast iron). Add the TVP and cook until it is dry, dark brown, and crispy, 8 to 10 minutes. Stir frequently to prevent burning. Remove the skillet from the heat and allow the TVP to cool. Store Baconish Bits in an airtight container about 1 week.

Beyond Bacon Recipes

Here are a few bonus recipes—they are not bacon, but they are pig-friendly! If you've ever enjoyed pulled pork, you are going to be amazed at how you can re-create the same texture with jackfruit smothered in luscious, spicy barbecue sauce! Saucy Spicy Chorizo (page 36) is great in any Mexican dish, or even just on a bun, Sloppy-Joe style. Seitan ham topped with a pineapple glaze (page 38) brings back childhood memories of my dad's pineapple-topped Christmas ham. And, of course, I've included Pigs in a Blanket (page 40), because that's how we like our pigs: cozy, safe, and warm.

Sweet and Spicy Barbecue Jackfruit

Makes 8 to 10 servings

Jackfruit is really having a moment among vegans. When pulled apart, the fruit has an uncanny appearance that resembles shredded or pulled meat. Having a mild flavor on its own, it lends itself well to savory dishes. You can find this Asian fruit canned in most Asian markets. You want to make sure to get the jackfruit in brine or water, not the sweet version in syrup.

2 tablespoons olive oil
1 medium onion, finely chopped
3 cloves garlic, minced
1 cup ketchup
2/3 cup maple syrup
1/4 cup brown sugar
3 teaspoons Sriracha sauce (more or less, depending on how spicy you like it)
3 teaspoons tamari
2 teaspoons Dijon mustard
1 teaspoon liquid smoke
1 teaspoon rice wine vinegar
2 (20-ounce) cans jackfruit in brine, drained, rinsed, and pulled apart
Whole-wheat burger buns, for serving

Heat the oil in a large pot over medium heat. Add the onion and garlic and sauté for 6 to 8 minutes, or until the onion is soft and translucent. Add the ketchup, maple syrup, brown sugar, Sriracha, tamari, mustard, liquid smoke, and rice wine vinegar. Stir to combine. Add the jackfruit and stir until it is thoroughly coated. Simmer for 10 to 15 minutes, or until the sauce thickens and the jackfruit breaks down further into shreds. Serve on the burger buns.

Saucy Spicy Chorizo

Makes 8 to 10 servings

This incredibly easy Mexican-style chorizo is made with TVP crumbles. It is delicious atop nachos, as a filling in tacos and burritos, in tofu scrambles, or even served on a bun, Sloppy-Joe style.

1 cup textured vegetable protein (TVP) (page 11)

1 cup hot vegetable broth

2 cups water

3 tablespoons tamari

2 tablespoons tomato paste

2 tablespoons red wine vinegar

2 cloves garlic, halved

1 tablespoon hot sauce, or to taste

2 teaspoons chili powder

1 teaspoon agave nectar

1 teaspoon smoked paprika

1 teaspoon ground cumin

1/2 teaspoon cayenne

1/2 teaspoon dried oregano

1/2 teaspoon ground black pepper

1/4 teaspoon ground cinnamon

2 tablespoons olive oil

Combine the TVP and hot broth in a large bowl. Cover the bowl and let the TVP steep 10 minutes, or until the liquid is absorbed. While the TVP is soaking, combine the water, tamari, tomato paste, red wine vinegar, garlic, hot sauce, chili powder, agave, smoked paprika, cumin, cayenne, oregano, pepper, and cinnamon in a blender. Blend until smooth.

Heat the oil in a skillet over medium–high heat. Add the TVP and sauté for 7 to 8 minutes, or until the TVP is lightly browned. Pour the sauce over the TVP and bring to a boil, then reduce to a simmer. Cook for 10 to 12 minutes, or until the liquid is reduced but the chorizo is still a bit saucy.

Pineapple-Glazed Seitan Ham
Makes 8 to 10 servings

Growing up, my family was the type that usually had a whole turkey and a baked ham on the table for holidays. This seitan ham is kind to the pigs and glazed with a sweet and smoky pineapple topping. The smell of it coming out of the oven reminds me of my dad's ham on Christmas morning. Serve slices on their own, in a sandwich, or even use this as a topping on the Hawaiian Pizza (page 157).

Seitan ham:
2 cups vital wheat gluten

3 tablespoons nutritional yeast

1/2 teaspoon garlic powder

1/2 teaspoon onion powder

1/2 teaspoon ground black pepper

1/4 teaspoon smoked paprika

1/4 teaspoon ground cloves

1 1/4 cups vegetable broth

3 tablespoons pineapple juice (reserved from the crushed pineapple used for glaze)

3 tablespoons maple syrup

2 tablespoons tomato paste

2 tablespoons tamari

1 tablespoon safflower or other neutral-tasting vegetable oil

1 1/2 teaspoons liquid smoke

Glaze:
2 tablespoons crushed pineapple in its own juice

1 tablespoon brown sugar

1 tablespoon vegan butter, melted

1 tablespoon Dijon mustard

1 tablespoon maple syrup

1/8 teaspoon liquid smoke

Seitan ham: Fit a steamer basket inside a large pot and fill with water to just below the basket line. Bring to a boil.

In a large bowl, combine the vital wheat gluten, nutritional yeast, garlic powder, onion powder, pepper, smoked paprika, and cloves. In another large bowl, whisk together the vegetable broth, pineapple juice, maple syrup, tomato paste, tamari, oil, and liquid smoke. Mix the wet ingredients into the dry ingredients, knead until they are well combined, and form the dough into a loaf shape.

Wrap the loaf in foil and place it in the steamer basket. Steam for 45 minutes, replacing water as needed. Allow the loaf to cool inside the foil. Preheat the oven to 350°F. Line a baking sheet with aluminum foil.

Glaze: Whisk together the crushed pineapple, brown sugar, butter, mustard, maple syrup, and liquid smoke in a small bowl. Place the seitan on the foil-lined sheet and, using a sharp paring knife, score a crisscross pattern all over the top, cutting about 1/4-inch deep. Brush the glaze all over the top and sides of the seitan. Bake the seitan for 20 minutes, then allow it to cool for 15 minutes before slicing and serving.

Pigs in a Blanket

Makes 6 servings

. . . .

My three-year-old son loves to eat these, although he doesn't agree with me that they look like little piggies in blankets. He says they should be called "Snakes in a Towel," but I don't think that sounds too great either. Whatever you call them, these tasty treats are pig-friendly, easy, and delicious.

Pigs in a Blanket:

1 (8-ounce) package vegan crescent rolls (Immaculate Baking brand and Pillsbury brand are vegan)
8 vegan hot dogs, cut into thirds (I prefer Lightlife Smart Dogs)

Dipping sauce:

1/4 cup apricot jam
3 tablespoons Dijon mustard
1 teaspoon tamari

Preheat the oven to 350°F. Unroll the crescents and separate them into 8 triangles. Using a sharp paring knife and starting at the point, cut each triangle lengthwise into 3 long triangles.

Place a piece of a veggie dog on the short side of a crescent triangle, then roll up toward the point. Repeat with the remaining veggie dogs and crescent triangles and arrange them on a large baking sheet, point-side down. Bake the Pigs in a Blanket for 14 to 16 minutes, or until golden brown.

While the hot dogs are baking, make the dipping sauce. In a small bowl, combine the jam, mustard, and tamari and mix well. Serve the warm hot dogs with dipping sauce.

Quiche Lorraine (page 60)

3

Breakfast

· ·

We all know that a side of vegan bacon makes any breakfast dish complete. Here, we've made breakfast even better by infusing every dish with baconish goodness. Now you don't have to settle for vegan bacon alongside your pancakes—you can have it *inside* your pancakes, your waffles, your tofu omelets, even your breakfast tacos. You can have it on top of your doughnuts, wrapped inside cinnamon rolls, and even baked into a coffee cake. Don't blame me if you can't sleep because you're too excited for your morning meal.

Bacon Pancake Dippers

Makes 4 servings

When I first saw recipes for these floating around the Internet, I thought it was a simple and ingenious way to combine our favorite sweet and savory breakfast elements. These dippers give you the perfect bacon-to-pancake ratio in each bite. This has been mathematically tested and proven true.

1 cup unbleached all-purpose flour
2 tablespoons baking powder
1/4 teaspoon salt
1/2 teaspoon ground cinnamon
1 cup plain unsweetened almond or soy milk
2 tablespoons safflower oil
1 tablespoon maple syrup
1/2 teaspoon vanilla extract
6 strips Tempeh Bacon (page 19), cut in half
Vegan butter (try Earth Balance) and additional maple syrup, for serving

Preheat the oven to the lowest temperature possible to keep the pancakes warm while you finish cooking them.

In a large bowl, whisk together the flour, baking powder, salt, and cinnamon. In a smaller bowl, whisk together the milk, oil, maple syrup, and vanilla. Add the wet ingredients to the dry ingredients and stir to combine, but do not overmix. Some lumps are fine.

Heat a griddle over medium-high heat and lightly mist it with nonstick cooking spray. Working in batches so as not to crowd your griddle, add the tempeh slices and brown them on one side, and then flip them over. Using a ladle, pour pancake batter over each tempeh slice. You want to barely cover each slice, as the batter will spread and expand enough to cover each one.

When the batter puffs up and you start to see bubbles on top, flip each dipper over and cook an additional minute or two until the other side is browned. Keep the dippers warm on a baking sheet in the oven until they are all finished cooking. Serve warm with butter and maple syrup.

Bacon-Stuffed French Toast
Makes 4 servings

This is another recipe that is perfect for brunch—a little sweet, a little savory, and filling enough to last you through lunchtime. Chickpea flour is used here to help create the perfect custardy batter for your toast.

    1 tablespoon olive oil
    8 slices vegan bacon (see note), halved, 1/4 cup Baconish Bits (page 32),
        or 8 slices store-bought vegan bacon
    4 ounces plain vegan cream cheese
    1 tablespoon strawberry jam (or your favorite fruit jam)
    8 slices whole-wheat bread
    2 cups plain soy creamer or almond or soy milk
    2 tablespoons cornstarch
    1/2 cup chickpea flour
    Vegan butter or nonstick cooking spray, for the pan
    Confectioners' sugar and maple syrup, for serving

Heat the oil in a large nonstick skillet over medium heat. Add the bacon slices and cook until they are crisped and browned. (Skip this step if you are using the already-prepared Baconish Bits.) Remove the bacon from the skillet and set aside.

In a small bowl, combine the vegan cream cheese and jam. (It doesn't have to be mixed perfectly smooth; in fact, I prefer when it's not.) Spread about 1 tablespoon of the cream cheese–jam mixture on each slice of bread. Place 4 half-slices of bacon on 4 of the bread slices, and then top with the remaining 4 slices of bread, cream cheese in the middle. You now have four cream cheese–bacon sandwiches. Reheat the same skillet that you used for the bacon over medium heat. Melt a small amount of butter in the pan or coat it with nonstick cooking spray.

In a large bowl, whisk together the soy creamer or milk, cornstarch, and chickpea flour. Dip each sandwich in the batter, making sure that both sides are well coated. Fry each sandwich in the pan for 3 to 4 minutes on each side, or until golden brown. Coat the pan with more butter or nonstick cooking spray as necessary. Serve the French toast sprinkled with confectioners' sugar and drizzled with maple syrup.

Note: Tempeh Bacon (page 19), Seitan Bacon (page 16), or Tofu Bacon (page 18) work best for this recipe. You can also use your favorite store-bought vegan bacon, if you prefer

Monte Cristo Waffles

with RASPBERRY SAUCE

Makes 4 servings

· ·

This recipe is inspired by the Monte Cristo sandwich, which is a batter-dipped ham and cheese sandwich that is served with confectioners' sugar and fruit preserves. In waffle form, it is the ultimate sweet-and-savory brunch treat.

Raspberry Sauce:

2 cups fresh or frozen raspberries

1/3 cup sugar

1 tablespoon cornstarch

1/4 cup water

Waffles:

2 cups unbleached all-purpose flour

1/2 cup cornmeal

1 teaspoon salt

3 teaspoons baking powder

2 cups plain unsweetened almond or soy milk

6 tablespoons aquafaba (page 8)

1/4 cup safflower oil

2 tablespoons maple syrup

1 cup diced Seitan Bacon (page 16), Tempeh Bacon (page 19), or Tofu
    Bacon (page 18)

1 1/2 cups vegan shredded mozzarella cheese

Confectioners' sugar, for serving

Raspberry Sauce: Combine the raspberries, sugar, cornstarch, and water in a small saucepan over medium heat. Bring to a simmer and cook until the raspberries break down and the sauce thickens, 6 to 8 minutes. Remove the sauce from the heat.

Waffles: Whisk together the flour, cornmeal, salt, and baking powder in a large bowl. In a separate bowl, whisk together the almond or soy milk, aquafaba, oil, and maple syrup. Pour the wet ingredients into the dry ingredients and stir until they are combined. Fold in the diced vegan bacon and cheese.

Heat a waffle iron. When it is ready, use a ladle to pour some waffle batter onto each square. Cook until the waffle is dark golden brown, 4 to 5 minutes. Transfer the waffles to a cooling rack while you cook the remaining batter, or serve immediately.

To serve, gently sift a spoonful of confectioners' sugar over the top of each waffle, then top with the raspberry sauce.

Bacon and Cheddar Scones

Makes 8 scones

. . . .

I used to think that I didn't like scones, but that was because I had only ever had bad, dry ones. This recipe makes a scone that is nice and crisp on the outside and tender, flaky, and buttery on the inside—just like it should be.

  2 cups unbleached all-purpose flour
  1 tablespoon baking powder
  1/2 teaspoon salt
  1/2 cup cold vegan butter, cut into 1/2-inch dice
  1 cup plain soy creamer
  1/2 cup Baconish Bits (page 32) or other vegan bacon, chopped
  1 cup vegan shredded cheddar cheese
  3 tablespoons chopped fresh chives

Preheat the oven to 450°F. Line a large baking sheet with parchment paper.

Whisk the flour, baking powder, and salt together in a large bowl. Using a pastry cutter, fork, or just your fingers, cut the butter into the flour until the mixture is coarse and pebbly. Stir in the creamer, bacon, cheddar, and chives, and mix until just blended.

Turn the dough out onto a lightly floured work surface. Gently knead the dough just enough for the mixture to be uniform, then shape into a circle about 7 inches in diameter and 1-inch thick. Use a sharp knife to cut the circle into 8 wedges. Gently place the wedges on the prepared baking sheet and bake 15 to 17 minutes, or until golden brown.

Biscuits with Southern Bacon Gravy
Makes about 10 servings

Growing up with a Southern family, I take my biscuits very seriously. They have to be soft and tender, flaky, and melt-in-your-mouth buttery—and ideally topped with some pepper-flecked white gravy. I'll tell you a secret, though: these biscuits are also amazing on their own with Sweet and Savory Bacon Jam (page 196). This recipe makes a lot, but both the biscuits and gravy can be frozen for future use. (See photo on page 54.)

Biscuits:

1 cup plain unsweetened almond or soy milk

1 tablespoon apple cider vinegar

3 cups unbleached all-purpose flour, plus more if needed

1 tablespoon baking powder

1 1/2 teaspoons sugar

1 teaspoon salt

1/2 teaspoon baking soda

1 cup (2 sticks) cold vegan butter, cut into small cubes

Gravy:

5 tablespoons vegan butter, divided

6 to 8 slices Tempeh Bacon (page 19) or your favorite vegan bacon

1/4 cup unbleached all-purpose flour

3 cups plain unsweetened almond or soy milk

1/2 teaspoon ground black pepper, or to taste

1 teaspoon salt, or to taste

Biscuits: Preheat the oven to 450°F. Line a large baking sheet with parchment paper and set aside.

In a small bowl or measuring cup, mix the almond or soy milk with the apple cider vinegar to create vegan buttermilk, then place it in the refrigerator to curdle and chill while you mix the other ingredients.

In a food processor, combine the flour, baking powder, sugar, salt, and baking soda and pulse a few times until combined. Add the butter, and pulse no more than 4 to 5 times, just until the butter is incorporated and the mixture resembles a coarse meal. Small, pea-size bits of butter are fine. Transfer the dough to a large bowl, add the buttermilk, and stir to combine.

Turn the dough out onto a floured work surface, then use your hands to knead just enough for the dough to come together in a loose ball. Use your hands to flatten and press the ball until it is about 1/2-inch thick. Using a floured 2 1/2-inch biscuit cutter, press down firmly to cut out rounds, then flip the rounds over and place them on the prepared baking sheet so that the flat side is on top—this will help the biscuits rise evenly. Bake the biscuits for 20 minutes, or until they are light golden brown on top.

Gravy: Melt 1 tablespoon of the butter in a large skillet (preferably cast iron) over medium-high heat. Add the bacon and cook until browned and crisped all over. Remove the bacon from the pan and set aside. When it is cool enough to handle, crumble the bacon into small pieces.

Reduce the heat to medium and melt the remaining 4 tablespoons of butter in the same skillet. Add the flour and whisk until thick and smooth, then add the almond or soy milk slowly, about 1/2 cup at a time, whisking constantly to incorporate. Add the pepper, salt, and reserved bacon, then bring the gravy to a simmer and cook 5 to 6 minutes until thickened, whisking often. Keep warm until ready to serve.

To serve, split one biscuit in half onto each plate and spoon gravy over the top. Top with additional crumbled vegan bacon, if desired.

Tip: If you get your hands on some Vegan Magic (page 201), this is one recipe where it works great. When making your gravy, replace some or all of the 5 tablespoons of butter with the same amount of Vegan Magic. Devour. Thank me later.

How to Make Great Biscuits

The key to successful biscuits is all about cold butter and not overworking your dough. You want your butter to stay as cold as possible; as it melts in the oven, it will create pockets of air, which will keep your biscuits light and flaky. Cube your butter, then put it back into the refrigerator to chill until you are ready to use it. Work as quickly as possible and try to get all your biscuits cut out without having to re-knead the leftover dough more than once.

Biscuits with Southern Bacon Gravy (page 52)

Breakfast Tacos (page 56)

Breakfast Tacos

Makes 4 servings

On a trip to Austin, Texas, several years ago, my husband and I were introduced to the genius of breakfast tacos. Tacos for breakfast! Actually, you can enjoy these for breakfast, lunch, or dinner. Or brunch. Or midnight snack. It's up to you. (See photo on page 55.)

Scramble:

1 pound extra-firm tofu, drained
1/4 cup nutritional yeast
1 1/2 teaspoons ground cumin
1/2 teaspoon turmeric
1/2 teaspoon onion powder
1 teaspoon salt
1/4 teaspoon ground black pepper
1/3 cup chopped Seitan Bacon (page 16) or your favorite vegan bacon
2 cloves garlic, chopped
1 small jalapeño, seeded and chopped
2 tablespoons olive oil

Potatoes:

3 cups frozen home fries
1 teaspoon smoked paprika
1 teaspoon ground cumin
1 teaspoon dried parsley
1/2 teaspoon garlic powder
1/2 teaspoon chili powder
3 tablespoons olive oil
Salt and ground black pepper, to taste

For serving:

8 (7-inch) corn tortillas
Sliced avocado
Salsa
Chopped fresh cilantro

Over the sink, use your hands to squeeze out the excess water from the tofu. Crumble the tofu into a large bowl, but not too finely—you still want to have some large chunks in there so that the consistency resembles scrambled eggs. Sprinkle the nutritional yeast, cumin, turmeric, onion powder, salt, and pepper over the tofu, then mix until the tofu seems evenly coated. Stir in the vegan bacon, garlic, and jalapeño.

Heat the oil in a nonstick skillet over medium-high heat. Add the tofu mixture and use a spatula to spread it out into an even layer in the skillet. Cook the tofu for 4 to 5 minutes undisturbed, so that it gets a nice brown crust on the bottom—resist the urge to stir it! Then use a wide spatula to flip the tofu over and cook another 5 to 6 minutes, until mostly browned all over.

In a large bowl, toss the frozen home fries with the smoked paprika, cumin, parsley, garlic powder, and chili powder. In another skillet (or the same skillet after you have cooked the tofu scramble), heat the oil over medium-high heat. Spread the potatoes in an even layer in the skillet and cook 5 to 7 minutes without stirring, so that they get nice and brown on the underside. Flip the potatoes and cook another 5 to 7 minutes until browned all over. Season with salt and pepper to taste.

To serve, heat the corn tortillas (see tip below), then fill each one with potatoes, tofu scramble, sliced avocado, salsa, cilantro, and any of your favorite taco fixings.

How to Heat the Tortillas

If you have a gas stove, heat the corn tortillas directly over the flame, using metal tongs. Place your tortillas, one at a time, directly on the burner, allowing the flame to lightly char the edges. Use metal tongs to move the tortillas around until they are heated and lightly charred all over. If you don't have a gas stove, you can heat the tortillas on the stove in a skillet.

Eggless McMuffins
Makes 4 servings

These breakfast sandwiches are easy to make and sure to become a go-to breakfast. After you cut out your "egg" rounds, you will end up with leftover scraps of tofu—feel free to toss them in with a tofu scramble later or scramble them with the leftover seasoning mix, which can be eaten right away, or (my favorite) added to a batch of fried rice later.

2 pounds extra-firm tofu, drained and pressed, or super-firm tofu, drained
2 tablespoons nutritional yeast
1/2 teaspoon salt
1/4 teaspoon turmeric
1/4 teaspoon onion powder
1/4 teaspoon garlic powder
Large pinch black salt
Ground black pepper, to taste
1 tablespoon olive oil
4 slices vegan cheddar cheese
4 English muffins, split
8 slices cooked Seitan Bacon (page 16) or your favorite vegan bacon
4 arugula leaves
Vegan mayonnaise, optional
Hot sauce, optional

Cut the tofu blocks in half along the short sides, so that you have two even rectangles from each block. Use a cookie or biscuit cutter or the rim of a glass that is the same diameter as the muffins, and cut out four tofu rounds—one from each rectangle.

In a small bowl, mix the nutritional yeast, salt, turmeric, onion powder, garlic powder, black salt, and pepper. Pour the mixture onto a plate, then dredge both sides of each tofu round in the mixture.

Heat the oil in a nonstick skillet over medium-high heat. Add the tofu rounds and cook for 4 to 5 minutes on each side, until crisp and golden brown. When you flip them over, place a cheese slice on each round so it melts as the other side cooks. Toast the English muffins.

Place a cooked tofu round on half of the muffins, top with bacon slices, arugula, and other condiments. Top with the remaining mushroom halves.

Quiche Lorraine

Makes 6 to 8 servings

. . . .

Back when I ate eggs, quiche was one of my favorite dishes. I rarely made my own, but I loved to order them for lunch or brunch. This quiche bakes up light, fluffy, and custardy, just the way I like it. Enjoy this for brunch with my favorite side dish, the mimosa. (See photo on page 42.)

    1/2 cup raw cashews
    14 ounces soft tofu, drained
    3 tablespoons cornstarch
    3 tablespoons nutritional yeast
    1 tablespoon white miso paste
    1 tablespoon Dijon mustard
    1/2 teaspoon salt
    1/2 teaspoon onion powder
    1 teaspoon olive oil
    1 cup chopped Seitan Bacon (page 16) or your favorite vegan bacon
    1 cup vegan shredded cheddar cheese
    1 (9-inch) Quick and Easy Whole-Wheat Pie Crust (page 61) or store-
        bought vegan pie crust
    Chopped fresh chives, for garnish

Preheat the oven to 350°F. In a blender or food processor, pulse the cashews until they are finely ground. Add the tofu, cornstarch, nutritional yeast, miso paste, mustard, salt, and onion powder, then blend again until the mixture is very smooth.

Heat the oil in a medium skillet over medium-high heat. Add the bacon pieces and cook until they are browned and crispy, 5 to 6 minutes.

In a large bowl, mix the tofu filling with the bacon and cheese. Pour the filling into the prepared pie crust and bake for 45 minutes, until deep golden brown on top. Cool on a wire rack for 20 minutes. Garnish with chopped fresh chives before serving.

Quick and Easy Whole-Wheat Pie Crust
Makes 1 (9-inch) pie crust

. . . .

This is a super quick and easy whole-wheat pie crust that is perfect for savory dishes like vegan quiche.

  1 1/4 cups whole-wheat flour
  1/4 teaspoon salt
  5 tablespoons cold vegan butter, cut into small cubes
  1/4 cup cold water

Pulse the flour, salt, and butter in a food processor until crumbly. With the processor on, slowly pour in the cold water and let it run until the dough forms a ball.

Transfer the dough onto a floured sheet of parchment paper. With a well-floured rolling pin, roll the dough out flat until it will fit in a 9-inch pie pan.

Use the parchment paper to lift up the dough and turn it over into the pie pan, then peel the paper away. Trim any excess dough from around the edges of the pie pan. The crust is now ready to fill and bake.

Bacon-Spinach Quiche
with SUN-DRIED TOMATOES
Makes 6 to 8 servings

. . . .

This quiche is like the BLT's fancier cousin. The sun-dried tomatoes really give it an extra flavor boost—I like to buy the kind packed in olive oil, because they have much better flavor. I love this quiche served at room temperature or slightly warmed, with a lightly dressed, simple green salad.

1/2 cup raw cashews

14 ounces soft tofu, drained

3 tablespoons cornstarch

3 tablespoons nutritional yeast

1 tablespoon white miso paste

1 tablespoon Dijon mustard

1/2 teaspoon salt

1/2 teaspoon onion powder

1 teaspoon olive oil

1/2 cup chopped Tempeh Bacon (page 19) or your favorite vegan bacon

1/4 cup sun-dried tomatoes, thinly sliced

3 cups baby spinach

1 (9-inch) Quick and Easy Whole-Wheat Pie Crust (page 61) or store-bought vegan pie crust

Preheat the oven to 350°F. In a blender or food processor, pulse the cashews until they are finely ground. Add the tofu, cornstarch, nutritional yeast, miso paste, mustard, salt, and onion powder. Blend again until the mixture is smooth.

Heat the oil in a nonstick skillet over medium heat. Add the bacon pieces and cook until they are browned all over, about 5 to 6 minutes. Add the sun-dried tomatoes and cook another minute. Add the spinach and cook until it is just wilted.

Transfer the bacon mixture to a large bowl, then add the tofu mixture and mix until well combined. Transfer the filling into the prepared pie crust and bake for 45 minutes, or until golden brown on top. Cool on a wire rack about 30 minutes before slicing.

Denver Omelet

Makes 4 servings

My husband is originally from the Denver area, although he says he never ate Denver omelets. He never liked eggs, even before he went vegan. I did, and omelets were a brunch-time favorite of mine. This is a classic, diner-style omelet stuffed full of bacon, peppers, and onions and is every bit as filling and satisfying as the "real" thing.

2 tablespoons olive oil, divided

1 small green bell pepper, finely chopped

1 small red onion, finely chopped

1 cup finely chopped Tempeh Bacon (page 19), Seitan Bacon (page 16),
   Tofu Bacon (page 18), or Roasted Chickpea Bacon (page 30)

1 pound silken or soft tofu, drained

1/2 cup chickpea flour

3 tablespoons cornstarch

3 tablespoons nutritional yeast

1/2 teaspoon turmeric

1/2 teaspoon onion powder

1/2 teaspoon garlic powder

1 teaspoon salt

Ground black pepper, to taste

Pinch black salt (optional, but recommended)

2 tablespoons vegan butter, divided

8 tablespoons vegan shredded cheddar cheese, divided

Preheat the oven to 200°F. Heat 1 tablespoon of the oil in a nonstick skillet over medium-high heat. Add the bell pepper, onion, and bacon and sauté for 8 to 10 minutes, or until the vegetables are soft and have begun to brown. Remove the vegetables and bacon from the skillet and set aside.

In a blender or food processor, combine the tofu, chickpea flour, cornstarch, nutritional yeast, the remaining 1 tablespoon oil, turmeric, onion powder, garlic powder, salt, pepper, and black salt (if using), and blend until the mixture is smooth. Stop to scrape the sides as necessary.

Melt 1/2 tablespoon of the vegan butter in a nonstick skillet over medium-high heat. Add 1/4 of the batter (about 1/2 cup), making a circle. Sprinkle 2 tablespoons of the vegan cheddar over the surface, then 1/4 of the bacon filling (about 1/2 cup). When the edges and most of the center of the omelet look dry, gently use your spatula to fold the omelet in half (if the middle is still slightly moist, it's okay). Use your spatula to gently slide the omelet out of the skillet onto an oven-safe plate or large baking sheet. Repeat this process with the remaining ingredients. Keep the cooked omelets warm in the oven while you cook the remaining omelets.

Chocolate Chip Coffee Cake

with CHERRIES AND BACON

Makes 10 to 12 servings

This crowd-pleasing coffee cake is incredibly moist and has little bits of savory bacon interspersed with chocolate chips and cherries, topped with a cinnamon-scented brown sugar streusel. Enjoy it with a cup of soy chai latte, which is what I like in the morning, or with your favorite cup of joe.

Streusel:

2 tablespoons safflower oil
3 tablespoons light brown sugar
2 tablespoons unbleached all-purpose flour
1 teaspoon ground cinnamon

Cake:

1 cup plain unsweetened almond or soy milk
1 tablespoon apple cider vinegar
2 cups unbleached all-purpose flour
1 cup sugar
1 tablespoon baking powder
1/2 teaspoon salt
1/2 cup canola oil
1 1/2 teaspoons vanilla extract
1/2 cup vegan chocolate chips
1/3 cup finely chopped Seitan Bacon (page 16), cooked
1 cup fresh or frozen cherries, pitted

Preheat the oven to 350°F. Spray a 9-inch round pan with nonstick cooking spray. Set aside. In a measuring cup, mix the almond or soy milk with the apple cider vinegar to create vegan buttermilk. Set aside and allow the milk to curdle while you prepare the rest of the cake.

Streusel: Use your fingers to mix the safflower oil, brown sugar, flour, and cinnamon in a small bowl. It will resemble wet sand. Set aside.

Cake: Whisk together the flour, sugar, baking powder, and salt in a large mixing bowl. Mix in the buttermilk, canola oil, and vanilla. Fold in the chocolate chips, chopped bacon, and cherries. Pour batter into the prepared pan, then use your hands to distribute the streusel evenly over the top.

Bake the cake for 45 minutes, or until a knife inserted in the cake comes out clean. Remove the cake from the oven and set aside to cool.

Variations: Use Tofu Bacon (page 18) or Tempeh Bacon (page 19) instead of the Seitan Bacon.

Maple-Bacon Doughnuts
Makes 12 doughnuts

Maple. Bacon. Doughnuts. The best three breakfast items, all rolled into one. If I could figure out a way to fill them with mimosas, my life would be complete. These are super moist, cakey doughnuts and, unlike the yeast-raised version, these are baked and so easy to make. Dangerously easy, I might say. Note that for this recipe, you will need a twelve-well, nonstick doughnut pan.

Doughnuts:
1/2 cup plain unsweetened almond or soy milk

1/2 teaspoon apple cider vinegar

1 cup plus 1 tablespoon unbleached all-purpose flour

2 teaspoons baking powder

1/4 teaspoon salt

1/2 teaspoon ground cinnamon

1/2 cup maple syrup

1 tablespoon sugar

3 tablespoons aquafaba (page 8) or other egg replacer of your choice, equivalent to 1 egg (page 13)

4 tablespoons safflower oil

Glaze:
1 cup confectioners' sugar

2 tablespoons maple syrup

1 to 2 tablespoons plain unsweetened almond or soy milk

1/4 cup Baconish Bits (page 32) or Coconut Bacon (page 21)

Preheat the oven to 350°F.

Doughnuts: Combine the almond or soy milk and apple cider vinegar to create vegan buttermilk in a small bowl. Set aside and allow the milk to curdle.

Whisk together the flour, baking powder, salt, and cinnamon in a large bowl. In another bowl, whisk together the maple syrup, sugar, aquafaba, safflower oil, and vegan buttermilk. Add the wet ingredients to the dry ingredients, and mix until they are combined.

Use a spoon to gently fill the doughnut pan. Each well should be about 2/3 to 3/4 full. Bake the doughnuts for 12 to 14 minutes, or until lightly golden. As soon as you remove them from the oven, invert the pans over a cooling rack to release the doughnuts. If you have any trouble getting the doughnuts out, gently tap the backside of the pan, or run a knife along the edge of the doughnuts to loosen them. Allow the doughnuts to cool completely before frosting.

Glaze: Combine the confectioners' sugar, maple syrup, and milk in a medium bowl, stirring to blend well. It should be thick and easily spreadable but not runny. If it's too thick, add more milk by the 1/2 teaspoon. If it's too thin, add a little more confectioners' sugar.

When the doughnuts are cool, dip each one halfway into the glaze, then place it on a cooling rack over a baking sheet lined with parchment paper, allowing the excess glaze to drip. Sprinkle 1/2 to 1 teaspoon Baconish Bits over each doughnut and lightly press so they stick to the glaze.

Bacon-Apple Fritters

Makes 36 fritters

. . . .

Look, this recipe has bacon, fried dough, and it's covered in confectioners' sugar. But it also has some apples in there, so that counts as a serving of fruit—right? This makes a batch for a large crowd, so have one or three of these deep-fried treats.

- 1 teaspoon plus 2 cups safflower oil, divided
- 5 to 6 slices Tempeh Bacon (page 19) or 1/2 cup Baconish Bits (page 32)
- 2 cups unbleached all-purpose flour
- 1/4 cup sugar
- 1 teaspoon baking powder
- 1/2 teaspoon salt
- 1/2 teaspoon ground cinnamon
- 1 cup plain unsweetened almond or soy milk
- 3 tablespoons aquafaba (page 8)
- 1/2 teaspoon vanilla extract
- 2 medium apples (any variety), peeled, cored, and cut into 1/4-inch pieces
- Confectioners' sugar, for dusting

If using the Tempeh Bacon, heat 1 teaspoon of the oil in a small skillet over medium-high heat. Add the Tempeh Bacon, then remove from the skillet and set aside. When the Tempeh Bacon is cool enough to handle, finely chop it or crumble it.

In a large mixing bowl, whisk together the flour, sugar, baking powder, salt, and cinnamon. In another bowl, whisk together the milk, aquafaba, and vanilla. Add the wet ingredients to the dry ingredients, then mix to combine. Fold in the apples and bacon. The batter will be thick and chunky.

Heat the remaining 2 cups of the oil in a large, deep-sided pot or skillet. When the oil is shimmering, drop rounded tablespoons of the batter into the oil. When the sides of the fritters are brown, gently flip each ball over and fry until brown on the other side. Working with two slotted wooden spoons is easiest for handling the fritters.

Remove the fritters from the oil and place them on a platter lined with paper towels to absorb the excess oil. Dust with confectioners' sugar. These are best eaten immediately.

Tip: If the fritters are getting dark too quickly on the outside, you may need to lower the heat.

Bacon Cinnamon Rolls

Makes 12 rolls

· ·

These soft, buttery, ooey-gooey little rounds of deliciousness do not qualify as health food. They are unapologetically decadent treats. But you're reading a book all about bacon, so you're not opposed to a little indulgence, are you? Note that for this recipe you will need a standing mixer with a dough hook attachment and a 9 x 13-inch baking pan.

Dough:

1 (1/4 ounce) packet active dry yeast

1/2 teaspoon plus 1/3 cup sugar, divided

1 cup plain unsweetened almond or soy milk, hot but not boiling

1/2 cup vegan butter

6 tablespoons aquafaba (page 8)

1 teaspoon vanilla extract

3/4 teaspoon salt

4 cups unbleached all-purpose flour

Filling:

3/4 cup brown sugar

2 tablespoons ground cinnamon

1/3 cup vegan butter, softened

3 tablespoons Baconish Bits (page 32)

Glaze:

1 cup confectioners' sugar

2 tablespoons plain or vanilla almond or soy milk

Dough: Stir the yeast and 1/2 teaspoon of the sugar into the hot milk in a small bowl. Set aside while you prepare the rest of the dough ingredients. In a standing mixer with the flat beater attachment, cream together the remaining 1/3 cup of sugar, butter, aquafaba, vanilla, and salt. Add the flour 1 cup at a time, mixing until incorporated. Fit the mixer with the dough hook attachment. Add the milk and yeast mixture. Mix until the dough pulls away from the sides of the bowl and forms a large ball around the hook. Transfer the dough to a large, lightly oiled bowl. Cover the dough and let it rise for 1 hour in a warm place, until it has about doubled in size.

Lightly grease a 9 x 13-inch baking pan. Transfer the dough to a lightly floured work surface and roll it out to a large rectangle approximately 16 inches wide by 12 inches long.

Filling: Combine the brown sugar, cinnamon, and softened butter in a medium bowl and mix well. Spread the cinnamon mixture evenly over the dough, leaving about an inch border around the edges. Sprinkle the Baconish Bits evenly all over the cinnamon mixture. Roll the dough from the widest side away from you, keeping the roll as tight as you can. Place the roll seam-side down. If the edges are a bit uneven, just pat them with your hands until they are square with the rest of the roll. Use a sharp serrated knife to cut 12 even slices. Place each roll cut-side up into the pan, so that you have 3 rows of 4 rolls each. Cover the rolls and let them rise for another 30 minutes.

Preheat the oven to 350°F. Bake the rolls for 20 to 25 minutes, or until golden brown. Remove the rolls from the oven and let them cool on a wire rack.

Glaze: In a small bowl, combine the confectioners' sugar and almond or soy milk and stir until smooth. Spoon or pour the glaze evenly all over the rolls in the pan. Serve warm or at room temperature.

Bonus Method for Bacon Cinnamon Rolls
Makes 5 large rolls

Cinnamon rolls are delicious, but sometimes you don't have the time or the patience for all that dough rising. You want your cinnamon rolls *now*. I understand! That is why I am including a quick and easy method to satisfy that cinnamon-y, baconish craving. Immaculate Baking and Trader Joe's both have vegan ready-to-bake cinnamon rolls.

1 package vegan ready-to-bake cinnamon rolls
5 slices Tempeh Bacon (page 19), uncooked

Remove each roll from the container and unroll it about 3/4 of the way. Place a strip of Tempeh Bacon on the dough, and then re-roll it closed, so your bacon strip is nicely rolled up inside. Place the Bacon Cinnamon Rolls on your prepared pan and bake according to package instructions. Glaze the rolls with the included frosting.

Baconish Granola
Makes about 3 cups

Making your own homemade granola is surprisingly easy, with an infinite number of ways you can customize it and make it your own. This granola recipe has the wonderful combination of maple syrup, coconut, almonds, and cranberries, with just a hint of smoky baconish flavor. Eat this with your favorite vegan milk, on top of some vegan yogurt, or as a topping for your favorite fruit crumble.

    1 cup unsweetened large-flake raw coconut
    1 tablespoon tamari
    1/2 teaspoon liquid smoke, divided
    1/2 cup sliced raw almonds
    2 1/2 cups rolled oats
    1/4 teaspoon salt
    1/3 cup maple syrup
    1/4 cup coconut oil
    1/4 teaspoon ground cinnamon
    1/2 teaspoon vanilla extract
    1 cup dried cranberries

Preheat the oven to 350°F. Line a large baking sheet with parchment paper and set aside.

In a medium bowl, combine the coconut, tamari, and 1/4 teaspoon of the liquid smoke. Mix to combine.

In a dry skillet over medium-high heat, lightly toast the almonds for 3 to 4 minutes, until lightly browned and fragrant. Transfer the almonds to a large mixing bowl, then in the same dry pan lightly toast the marinated coconut for 3 to 4 minutes, until lightly browned and fragrant. Add the coconut to the bowl with the almonds.

Spread the oats out on the prepared baking sheet and toast in the oven for 10 minutes, until lightly browned. Add the oats to the almonds and coconut, along with the salt. Mix well and set aside. Keep the parchment-lined baking sheet to bake the granola.

In a small saucepan, combine the maple syrup, oil, the remaining 1/4 teaspoon liquid smoke, cinnamon, and vanilla. Bring to a simmer, whisking constantly. Pour the syrup mixture over the oat mixture and quickly stir everything so that it is evenly combined.

Spread the granola out on the baking sheet in an even but compact layer, so that it sticks together.

Bake for 10 minutes. Remove the granola from the oven and stir in the cranberries. Allow the mixture to cool completely before breaking it up into clusters. This will keep, stored in an airtight container, for up to 2 weeks.

Tip: Feel free to experiment with the dried fruit in this recipe, by combining or replacing the cranberries with dried blueberries, dried apples, raisins, and so on.

Loaded Potato Soup with Bacon (page 78)

Soups

Question: Which types of soup are made better by adding a little bacon? Answer: All of them! Here are just a few of my favorite soups that go best with bacon. These recipes are warm and comforting and so loaded with flavor, you'll never believe that they don't include any meat or dairy. Creamy, satisfying loaded potato, sultry smoky split pea, summery corn chowder, luscious miso ramen, spicy chili, and white bean soup loaded with fresh herbs.

Feel free to mix and match with any of the vegan bacons—you can't go wrong.

Loaded Potato Soup with Bacon

Makes 4 servings

....

This potato soup is hearty, comforting, super easy to make, and loaded with all your favorite potato bar fixings. Eat it when there's a chill in the air, and you'll feel warm and cozy.

2 tablespoons olive oil

1 medium onion, finely chopped

2 cloves garlic, minced

4 russet potatoes (2 pounds), peeled and cut into 3/4-inch dice

2 cups vegetable broth

2 cups plain unsweetened almond or soy milk

1 teaspoon dried rosemary

Salt and ground black pepper, to taste

For serving:

Vegan sour cream

Fresh chives, chopped

Vegan shredded cheddar cheese

Cooked chopped vegan bacon (any kind) or Baconish Bits (page 32)

Heat the oil in a large pot over medium-high heat. Add the onion and garlic and sauté for 5 minutes, or until softened. Add the potatoes, broth, almond or soy milk, and rosemary. Bring the soup to a boil, then reduce to a simmer and cook for about 30 minutes, or until the potatoes are easily pierced with a fork.

Use an immersion blender to puree the soup to the desired consistency. It doesn't have to be completely smooth; personally, I like to leave a few chunks of potato for texture. If you don't have an immersion blender, you can ladle about half of the soup into a regular blender to puree, then transfer it back to the pot. Season with salt and pepper to taste.

To serve, divide the soup evenly into four bowls. Add a dollop of vegan sour cream and a sprinkle of fresh chives, vegan cheddar, and bacon or Baconish Bits to each serving.

Smoky Split Pea Soup with Bacon
Makes 4 to 6 servings

Split pea soup is often made with smoked ham, but this recipe proves that meat is totally unnecessary to get a deliciously smoky, flavorful, satisfying soup. It is wonderfully smoky and baconish on its own, but, of course, you should top it with a sprinkle of your favorite vegan bacon.

 2 tablespoons olive oil, plus more for drizzling
 2 medium carrots, cut into 1/4-inch dice
 1 medium onion, cut into 1/4-inch dice
 3 cloves garlic, minced
 2 tablespoons smoked paprika, plus more for serving
 1 teaspoon dried thyme
 1 dried bay leaf
 1 teaspoon salt
 1 teaspoon ground black pepper
 1 teaspoon liquid smoke
 1 pound dried split peas
 6 cups vegetable broth or water
 1/2 cup chopped Shiitake Mushroom Bacon (page 26) or Carrot Bacon (page 29), for serving

Heat the oil in a large pot over medium-high heat. Add the carrots and onion and cook for 5 minutes, stirring occasionally, until the vegetables are softened and the onion is translucent. Add the garlic and cook 1 minute longer.

Stir in the smoked paprika, thyme, bay leaf, salt, pepper, and liquid smoke. Add the split peas and broth. Turn the heat up to high and bring the soup to a boil. Once the soup is boiling, reduce to a simmer and cook for 40 to 45 minutes, or until the peas are tender. Remove and discard the bay leaf before serving.

To serve, ladle the soup into bowls then drizzle a small amount of high-quality olive oil on top. Top each serving with a little extra smoked paprika and the chopped bacon.

Corn Chowder with Coconut Bacon
Makes 4 servings

. . . .

This chowder is the perfect segue from summer to fall—sweet corn with earthy potatoes, balanced by just a touch of heat from the jalapeños and perfectly complemented by crispy, smoky coconut bacon. It's so good and easy to make, you'll want to eat it year-round.

    4 tablespoons olive oil
    1 medium yellow onion, finely chopped
    1 to 2 jalapeños, seeded and minced (depending on how spicy you like it)
    4 cups fresh or frozen corn kernels, thawed if frozen
    1 pound Yukon gold potatoes, cut into 1/2-inch dice (about 3 potatoes)
    1/2 teaspoon salt
    Ground black pepper, to taste
    1/2 teaspoon dried thyme
    1/2 teaspoon dried oregano
    1/2 teaspoon paprika
    3 cups vegetable broth
    1/4 cup Coconut Bacon (page 21), for serving

Heat the oil in a large pot over medium heat. Add the onion and jalapeño and cook for 5 to 8 minutes, stirring occasionally, until the vegetables are soft.

Add the corn and potatoes, cook for 3 to 4 minutes, then add the salt, pepper to taste, thyme, oregano, and paprika. Stir to coat the vegetables thoroughly.

Add the vegetable broth and bring the soup to a boil, then cover and simmer over low heat for 15 to 20 minutes, or until the potatoes are tender. Taste and season with additional salt and pepper, if needed.

Carefully ladle about half of the soup into a blender and puree. Return the blended soup to the pot and mix well. (Alternatively, use an immersion blender to blend some of the soup. You want it to be thick but still have whole chunks of corn and potato.) Serve and top with a generous sprinkle of Coconut Bacon.

Miso Ramen Soup with Smoked Tofu
and KING TRUMPET MUSHROOM BACON
Makes 4 servings

. . . .

We used to live just a block from a very popular ramen restaurant named Chuko. Their veggie ramen is one of the best I have ever tasted. It has a rich, flavorful broth with a touch of sweetness that tastes to me of mellow white miso paste and mirin wine. It is the inspiration for my easy at-home version here.

10 ounces dried ramen noodles

2 tablespoons safflower oil

1 medium onion, coarsely chopped

2 cloves garlic, coarsely chopped

1 (1-inch) piece fresh ginger, peeled and grated

1 ounce dried shiitake mushrooms

6 cups vegetable broth

1/2 cup white miso paste

1/4 cup mirin

1 tablespoon tamari (more or less, depending on the saltiness of your broth)

1 teaspoon rice vinegar

1 teaspoon toasted sesame oil

Additional toppings:
Smoked tofu or cooked Tofu Bacon (page 18), cut into 1/2-inch dice

King Trumpet Mushroom Bacon (page 25), coarsely chopped

Green onions, thinly sliced

Napa cabbage, shredded

Garlic chili sauce, optional

Bring 1 quart of water to a boil in a large pot. Add the noodles and gently separate them as they begin to soften. Reduce the heat to medium and boil gently for 3 to 4 minutes, or until the noodles are tender. Drain the noodles and rinse them under cold water.

Heat the safflower oil in a medium pot over medium heat. Add the onion, garlic, and ginger and cook for 5 to 6 minutes, until the vegetables are soft and just barely starting to brown. Add the dried mushrooms and vegetable broth. Bring the soup to a boil, then reduce the heat to a simmer and cook for 30 minutes. Strain, reserving the broth. Discard the vegetables.

Transfer the strained broth back to the pot over low heat. Add the miso paste, mirin, and tamari. Simmer for 10 minutes, then stir in the rice vinegar and sesame oil.

Divide the noodles evenly into 4 serving bowls. Pour the hot broth evenly over each serving of noodles. Top each serving with tofu, King Trumpet Mushroom Bacon, green onions, and shredded cabbage. Serve with garlic chili sauce on the side, if desired.

Baconish Bean Chili

Makes 4 to 6 servings

. . . .

Every vegan will at some point be asked the question, "So where do you get your protein?" I like to answer, "Chili." This chili is protein-packed, smoky, and spicy. You will want to eat it year-round.

2 tablespoons olive oil, plus more if necessary

1 medium onion, coarsely chopped

3 cloves garlic, minced

6 slices Tempeh Bacon (page 19), finely chopped

1 (11-ounce) package vegan beef crumbles, thawed (I recommend Be-
    yond Meat or Gardein brands)

2 tablespoons chili powder

2 teaspoons ground cumin

1 1/2 teaspoons smoked paprika

1 teaspoon cayenne

1 teaspoon salt, or to taste

1 teaspoon ground black pepper

1 (28-ounce) can plus 1 (15-ounce) can crushed tomatoes

1 (15-ounce) can pinto beans, drained and rinsed

1 (15-ounce) can black beans, drained and rinsed

1 (12-ounce) bottle medium-bodied beer

1 teaspoon vegan Worcestershire sauce

1 teaspoon brown sugar

1/2 teaspoon liquid smoke

For serving:

Vegan sour cream

Sliced green onions

Sliced avocado

Vegan shredded cheddar (I recommend Daiya brand)

Lime wedges

Hot sauce

Heat the oil in a large pot over medium heat. Add the onion and garlic and cook 3 to 4 minutes. Add the Tempeh Bacon and vegan beef crumbles, and cook, stirring often, 4 to 5 minutes. If you find that the crumbles are sticking to the pot too much, add another tablespoon of oil.

Add the chili powder, cumin, paprika, cayenne, salt, and pepper and stir well, scraping the bottom of the pot to prevent sticking. Add the tomatoes, pinto beans, black beans, beer, Worcestershire, brown sugar, and liquid smoke. Stir well, bring to a boil, then simmer for 30 minutes.

To serve, ladle the chili into serving bowls and top with a dollop of vegan sour cream, sliced green onions, sliced avocado, a sprinkle of vegan cheddar shreds, a lime wedge for squeezing, and a dash or two of hot sauce.

White Bean and Bacon Soup

Makes 4 servings

. . . .

This is a smoky, hearty, flavorful bean soup that is brightened up with fresh herbs and just a bit of lemon juice before serving. I love to eat it with a nice, crusty, fresh baguette.

    3 tablespoons olive oil
    1 medium onion, finely chopped
    2 ribs celery, finely chopped
    1 large carrot, finely chopped
    5 slices Seitan Bacon (page 16), coarsely chopped
    2 cloves garlic, minced
    2 (15-ounce) cans cannellini beans, rinsed and drained
    4 cups vegetable broth
    1 dried bay leaf
    1 teaspoon smoked paprika
    1/2 teaspoon liquid smoke
    1 tablespoon tomato paste
    1 tablespoon fresh rosemary, finely chopped, plus more for serving
    1 tablespoon fresh thyme leaves, plus more for serving
    1 teaspoon salt
    1/2 teaspoon ground black pepper
    2 tablespoons fresh lemon juice
    1/4 cup Carrot Bacon (page 29), for serving

Heat the oil in a large pot over medium heat. Add the onion, celery, and carrot, and cook 5 minutes, until the vegetables have softened. Add the chopped Seitan Bacon and cook another 4 minutes, until lightly browned. Add the garlic and cook another minute.

Add the cannellini beans, broth, bay leaf, smoked paprika, liquid smoke, tomato paste, rosemary, thyme, salt, and pepper. Stir well and bring to a boil, then reduce the heat and simmer for 20 minutes. Add the lemon juice and stir to combine. Remove and discard the bay leaf before serving.

Divide the soup evenly into four bowls and top each serving with Carrot Bacon and a sprinkle of fresh herbs.

French Lentil Salad (page 102)

5

Salads

· ·

Vegan bacon is a lot healthier than animal-based bacon, but this section will make you feel even more virtuous while eating it. These salads have plenty of protein and fresh vegetables and are satisfying without being heavy. If you think that vegans only eat boring green salads, then this section will convince you that even salads can be hearty and delicious and loaded with baconish flavor. There's nothing boring about any of these.

Cobb Salad with Eggplant Bacon
Makes 4 servings

· ·

A traditional Cobb salad includes chicken, bacon, egg, and cheese. Not exactly vegan fare. But I've created a vegan-friendly version here that is incredibly flavorful, colorful, and totally satisfying. This is no wimpy side salad; this is a main course right here.

1 small head romaine lettuce, washed and cut into bite-size pieces
   (about 7 cups)
1 cup watercress, tough stems removed
1 cup Eggplant Bacon (page 22) or other vegan bacon
1 Hass avocado, peeled, pitted, and thinly sliced
1/2 cup grape or cherry tomatoes, halved
1 cup cooked or canned great Northern beans, drained and rinsed
1/2 cup fresh or frozen corn kernels, thawed if frozen
Vegan Blue Cheese Dressing (page 96)

Place the romaine in a large salad bowl or other serving dish. Arrange the watercress, Eggplant Bacon, avocado, tomatoes, beans, and corn artfully on top of the romaine. Top with the dressing. Toss the salad immediately before serving.

Spinach and Fresh Fig Salad
WITH WARM BACON-SHALLOT VINAIGRETTE
Makes 4 servings

To me, this is a perfect fall salad—lush, juicy figs; tangy, sweet, mustardy dressing; and smoky Baconish Bits. This recipe will make about a cup of the dressing, so you will have plenty left over to use later. I love to put the dressing on while it's still warm, but, of course, it's also delicious cold or at room temperature.

    4 tablespoons olive oil, divided
    1 large shallot, minced
    1/4 cup apple cider vinegar
    1 tablespoon Dijon mustard
    2 tablespoons agave nectar
    2 tablespoons Baconish Bits (page 32)
    Salt and ground black pepper, to taste
    5 ounces baby spinach leaves
    8 small fresh figs, washed and quartered

Heat 1 tablespoon of the oil in a medium skillet over medium-high heat. Add the shallot and cook for 3 to 4 minutes, until softened but not browned. Remove the pan from the heat, then whisk the apple cider vinegar, mustard, agave, and the remaining 3 tablespoons of oil directly into the pan. Add the Baconish Bits and stir to combine. Season with salt and pepper to taste. Divide the spinach leaves into equal portions onto four plates and arrange two figs, quartered, on top of each salad. Top with the vinaigrette.

Wedge Salad with Vegan Blue Cheese
DRESSING *and* BACONISH BITS
Makes 4 servings

. . . .

I used to love blue cheese dressing when I still ate dairy. This might sound like an odd list of ingredients, but they come together to give that sharp, tangy, slightly funky, cheesy creaminess of blue cheese. This dressing is really satisfying and is also great as a dipping sauce for crudités or vegan Buffalo wings. There will be leftover dressing, but it will keep well in the refrigerator for at least a week when stored in a container with a tight-fitting lid.

Vegan Blue Cheese Dressing:
1 cup vegan mayonnaise
3 tablespoons lemon juice
1 tablespoon white miso paste
1 1/2 teaspoons apple cider vinegar
1 teaspoon nutritional yeast
1/2 teaspoon kelp granules
1/2 teaspoon tahini
1/4 teaspoon garlic powder
1/4 teaspoon onion powder
7 ounces extra-firm tofu (about 1/2 block), drained and crumbled
Salt and ground black pepper, to taste

For serving:
1 small head iceberg lettuce, cored and quartered
1/4 cup Baconish Bits (page 32)

In a medium mixing bowl, whisk together the mayonnaise, lemon juice, miso paste, apple cider vinegar, nutritional yeast, kelp, tahini, garlic powder, and onion powder. Fold in the crumbled tofu and season with salt and pepper. To serve, place the lettuce wedges on 4 salad plates or shallow bowls. Spoon on the desired amount of dressing over each wedge of lettuce and sprinkle with Baconish Bits.

Tip: You don't need to press the tofu for this recipe. Just try to squeeze out as much water as you can with your hands.

Broccoli and Tempeh Bacon Salad
Makes 4 servings

. . . .

This recipe was contributed by my dear friend Wendy, who fell in love with this salad from her local food co-op and re-created it at home. She shared the recipe with me, and I fell in love with it, too. Every bite is the perfect combination of salty, sweet, chewy, and crunchy.

8 slices Tempeh Bacon (page 19), cooked and finely chopped or crumbled
1 cup chopped broccoli
1/2 cup grape tomatoes, quartered
1/2 cup red onion, minced
1/4 cup raisins
3 tablespoons roasted sunflower seeds
1 tablespoon agave nectar
1/2 cup vegan mayonnaise

Combine the bacon, broccoli, tomatoes, onion, raisins, and sunflower seeds in a large bowl. Drizzle the agave nectar over the broccoli mixture, then add the mayonnaise and mix well. For the best flavor, refrigerate at least 20 minutes before serving.

German-Style Potato Salad with Bacon

Makes 4 servings

German-style potato salad differs from the usual mayonnaise-laden variety with a dressing that is vinegar- and mustard-based. It's got a little more zing to it, and the bacon lends some added smoke and savoriness.

2 pounds yellow or red potatoes, halved (quartered if large)
3 tablespoons olive oil
1/2 red onion, finely chopped
1/2 cup chopped Tempeh Bacon (page 19) or your favorite vegan bacon
3 tablespoons apple cider vinegar
2 tablespoons whole-grain mustard
1 tablespoon agave nectar
3 tablespoons chopped fresh parsley
1 teaspoon salt
Ground black pepper, to taste

Place the potatoes in a large pot with enough salted, cold water to cover them by 2 inches. Bring to a boil and cook for 10 to 15 minutes, or until the potatoes are tender. Drain the potatoes, and when they are cool enough to handle, cut them into 1-inch chunks. Set aside.

Heat the oil in a medium skillet over medium-high heat. Add the onion and bacon and sauté for 5 minutes, or until the bacon is browned and the onion is softened.

In a large mixing bowl, whisk together the apple cider vinegar, mustard, agave, parsley, salt, and pepper. Stir in the onion and bacon, including any oil still in the pan. Add the potatoes and toss to coat. Taste and season with additional salt and pepper, if necessary. Serve at room temperature or (even better) slightly warm.

French Lentil Salad

with Tofu Bacon Lardons

Makes 6 servings

. . . .

This simple lentil salad with a tangy, mustardy vinaigrette takes me back to my days of being a student in Paris. Enjoy it with a hunk of baguette and some vegan butter. And if you want to be really French, with a glass of wine. Who cares if it's lunchtime?

Lentils:

1 cup green French lentils

4 cups water

1 clove garlic, halved

1 dried bay leaf

Salad:

2 tablespoons olive oil

2 medium shallots, halved and sliced paper thin

2 cloves garlic, minced

2 small carrots, cut into 1/8-inch thick slices

1/2 cup Tofu Bacon, cut into 1/4-inch lardons (page 18)

1 teaspoon fresh thyme leaves

1/4 cup chopped fresh parsley

Dressing:

1/4 cup olive oil

1 tablespoon Dijon mustard

2 tablespoons red wine vinegar

Salt and ground black pepper, to taste

Frisée or other lettuce leaves, for serving

Lentils: Combine the lentils, water, garlic, and bay leaf in a medium pot. Bring to a boil, then lower the heat to a simmer and cook, covered, for 15 to 20 minutes, or until the lentils are tender. Drain the lentils and remove and discard the garlic and bay leaf before serving.

Salad: Heat the oil in a large skillet over medium heat. Add the shallots, garlic, carrots, and Tofu Bacon lardons and cook, stirring occasionally for 8 to 10 minutes, or until the vegetables are soft and beginning to brown. Add the thyme and parsley, and cook 1 minute longer. Mix in the lentils.

Dressing: Whisk together the oil, mustard, and red wine vinegar in a small bowl. Pour the dressing over the lentil mixture and toss to combine. Season with salt and pepper to taste. Arrange the frisée or lettuce leaves on plates, then top with the lentil salad.

Fried Green Tomato BLT (page 112)

Sandwiches

In the words of the ingenious Liz Lemon, "All of humankind has one thing in common: the sandwich. I believe that all anyone really wants in this life is to sit in peace and eat a sandwich." I would add to that, to sit in peace and eat a baconish sandwich. Of course, vegan bacon goes well on any sandwich, but the ones in this chapter were selected because of the way they showcase their baconishness. The salty smokiness of the bacon is the perfect complement to cheesy grilled sandwiches, hearty veggie burgers, and plump veggie dogs or to simple crisp lettuce and fresh tomato on a classic BLT.

The Famous Coconut BLT
Makes 4 sandwiches

This recipe will make any vegan-bacon skeptic a true believer. It is my absolute favorite bacon to use for the best BLTs ever. Because Coconut Bacon will become less crisp the longer you store it, I recommend making it just ahead of preparing your sandwiches.

8 slices sandwich bread
Vegan mayonnaise
2 cups Coconut Bacon (page 21)
1 large ripe tomato, sliced
Lettuce leaves, washed and patted dry

Spread each slice of bread with a generous amount of mayonnaise. Top the mayonnaise with about 1/2 cup of the Coconut Bacon per sandwich, followed by slices of tomato and lettuce leaves. Top each sandwich with the remaining bread slices. Cut each sandwich with a serrated bread knife and serve immediately.

Black Bean Barbecue Bacon Cheeseburgers
Makes 8 burgers

· ·

If I have one major pet peeve, it's veggie burgers that are mushy and fall apart when you try to eat them. I went through countless tests to come up with a burger recipe that holds together and has plenty of flavor and texture. These are big, hearty, restaurant-size burgers that are loaded with spicy seasonings and perfect with some vegan bacon, cheese, and all your other favorite toppings.

  1 medium onion, quartered
  12 ounces mushrooms (buttons, shiitakes, porcinis, or a mixture)
  1 medium jalapeño, seeded and quartered
  1 (15-ounce) can black beans, drained and rinsed, divided
  1 cup cooked brown rice
  3 tablespoons barbecue sauce, plus more for glazing
  2 tablespoons tomato paste
  1 teaspoon salt
  1 teaspoon ground black pepper
  1/2 cup cornmeal
  1/2 cup vital wheat gluten
  1/4 cup Baconish Bits (page 32)
  8 slices vegan cheese
  8 whole-wheat hamburger buns
  8 slices Tempeh Bacon (page 19), cooked
  Toppings: Lettuce, sliced tomato, sliced onion, sliced avocado, pickles, ketchup

Preheat the oven to 400°F. Line a baking sheet with parchment paper.

In a food processor, combine the onion, mushrooms, and jalapeño and pulse 10 to 12 times, until the vegetables are coarsely chopped. Transfer the vegetables to a large mixing bowl.

Transfer 1 cup of the black beans into the food processor, then add the rice, barbecue sauce, tomato paste, salt, and pepper. Pulse about 10 to 12 times, until the beans are coarsely chopped and the ingredients are combined. Transfer to the mixing bowl with the onion mixture and add the remaining 1/2 cup black beans, cornmeal, wheat gluten, and Baconish Bits. Mix with your hands until well combined.

Use a 1/2-cup measure to scoop the mixture and use your hands to form the mixture into patties. Arrange the patties on the prepared baking sheet, and glaze the barbecue sauce over the top of each patty. Bake the patties for 30 minutes, then flip them and bake another 10 minutes. Place a slice of cheese on top of each burger, then return them to the oven for 2 to 3 minutes, or until the cheese is melted. Place each burger on a bun and garnish with a slice of Tempeh Bacon and toppings of your choice.

Apple, Bacon, and Cheddar Grilled Cheese

Makes 1 sandwich

. . . .

If you've ever had a slice of cheddar on your apple pie, then you already know that apple and cheddar make a great combination. What makes it even better? Bacon, of course! (Have you not learned that yet?) For another twist, try making this sandwich with the Sweet and Savory Bacon Jam (page 196).

   1 tablespoon vegan butter
   2 slices sandwich bread
   2 slices vegan cheddar cheese
   3 slices cooked Tempeh Bacon (page 19) or 1 to 2 tablespoons Sweet
      and Savory Bacon Jam (page 196)
   1/2 green apple, cored and sliced paper thin

Heat a large nonstick skillet or grill pan over medium heat. Spread the butter on each slice of bread. Place 1 slice of bread, buttered side down, on the hot pan. Add a slice of cheese, arrange the bacon slices on top of the cheese, then place the apple slices on top of the bacon. Top with the second slice of cheese, then place the other slice of bread, buttered side up, on top of the sandwich and press with a spatula to help flatten it and melt the cheese. After a couple of minutes, when the bottom slice of bread is browned, carefully flip the sandwich over to brown the other slice.

Fried Green Tomato BLT
Makes 4 sandwiches

. . . .

This Southern twist on the classic BLT is dressed up with Cajun seasonings and topped with Bacon Remoulade. Green tomatoes are easiest to find at the beginning and end of summer. (See photo on page 104.)

  1/4 cup cornmeal
  1 teaspoon Cajun seasoning blend
  1 large green tomato, cut into 4 (1/2-thick) slices
  Salt and ground black pepper, to taste
  2 tablespoons olive oil
  Bacon Remoulade (page 113)
  4 sandwich buns
  8 slices vegan bacon (any kind), cooked
  1 cup shredded romaine or iceberg lettuce

Mix the cornmeal and Cajun seasoning blend in a medium bowl. Season the tomato slices with salt and pepper, then dip each slice into the cornmeal, pressing down to ensure the coating sticks to both sides.

Heat the oil in a large skillet over medium-high heat. Add the tomato slices and cook for 3 to 4 minutes on each side, or until browned. Spread the Bacon Remoulade inside the top and bottom of each sandwich bun. For each sandwich, layer the fried green tomato, bacon slices, and lettuce on the bottom half of each bun, then top with the top half.

Bacon Remoulade

Makes about 1/2 cup

Use this on anything that needs a little Cajun, baconish kick.

1/2 cup vegan mayonnaise
2 teaspoons Dijon mustard
2 tablespoons finely chopped cornichons or sweet gherkins
1 tablespoon Baconish Bits (page 32)
1/4 teaspoon dried parsley
1/4 teaspoon dried oregano
1/4 teaspoon paprika
Tabasco brand hot sauce or other vinegar-based hot sauce
Salt and ground black pepper, to taste

Combine all the ingrediets in a medium bowl. Taste and adjust the seasonings, if necessary. Cover and refrigerate any unused portion.

The More-to-Love Elvis Sandwich

Makes 1 sandwich

I don't think it's nice to call people "fat," so I decided to rename this sandwich the "More-to-Love Elvis." Whatever you call it, the combination of peanut butter, vegan bacon, and banana is undeniably good. Are you going to argue with the King?

1 tablespoon vegan butter
2 slices sandwich bread
2 to 3 tablespoons peanut butter (I recommend crunchy)
2 to 4 slices Tempeh Bacon (page 19) or Seitan Bacon (page 16)
1/2 medium banana, cut into 1/4-inch slices
Agave nectar, for drizzling, optional

Heat a nonstick skillet or grill pan over medium heat. Spread the butter on both slices of bread. Spread the peanut butter on the opposite sides of each slice. Place 1 slice of bread, buttered side down, on the hot pan. Arrange the bacon slices on the peanut butter, then arrange the banana slices on top of the bacon. Place the other slice of bread, buttered side up, on top of the sandwich and press with a spatula to help flatten it. After a couple of minutes, when the bottom slice of bread is browned, carefully flip the sandwich over to brown the top slice.

Grilled Bacon Kim-Cheese

Makes 1 sandwich

It's a grilled cheese with kimchi! A kim-*cheese* sandwich! If you have not yet discovered the amazing combination that is warm, melted cheddar and spicy, crunchy kimchi, well, then you are in for an awakening. Throw some vegan bacon on there, and you've hit nirvana.

1 tablespoon vegan butter

2 slices sandwich bread

2 slices vegan cheddar cheese

3 slices Tempeh Bacon (page 19) or other vegan bacon

3 heaping tablespoons Quick and Easy Kimchi (page 117) or store-bought vegan kimchi

Heat a nonstick skillet or grill pan. Spread the butter on 2 slices of bread. Place 1 slice, buttered side down, on the hot pan. Add a slice of cheese, top the cheese with the bacon slices and kimchi, then top the kimchi with the second slice of cheese. Place the other slice of bread, buttered side up, on top of the sandwich and press with a spatula to help flatten it and melt the cheese. After a couple of minutes, when the bottom slice of bread is browned, carefully flip the sandwich over to brown the top slice.

Quick and Easy Kimchi
Makes about 6 cups

....

In NYC, kimchi is fairly easy to find even in most neighborhood grocery stores, but if it's not readily available where you live, or if you're just in a pinch and having a kimchi emergency, you can make a quick version at home. I'm not claiming this is the most authentic version, but it's pretty darn tasty. If buying store-bought kimchi, be sure to read the labels because some brands aren't vegan.

1 medium head napa cabbage (about 2 pounds)

2 tablespoons coarse sea salt

1/4 cup gochugaru (see Note)

3 cloves garlic, minced

1 tablespoon grated fresh ginger

3 tablespoons tamari or soy sauce

2 tablespoons rice vinegar

2 teaspoons sugar

3 green onions, cut into 2- to 3-inch pieces

1 tablespoon sesame oil

2 tablespoons toasted sesame seeds or gomasio mix (black sesame seeds with sea salt)

Cut off the stem base of the cabbage, then cut each leaf in half vertically, then into 2- to 3-inch pieces. Toss the leaves with the salt in a large bowl, then let sit for 30 to 60 minutes, depending on how much time you have, tossing the leaves halfway through to ensure even seasoning. Wash and drain the cabbage thoroughly in a colander, then press out as much excess water as you can.

Toss the cabbage with the gochugaru until it is evenly coated. In a small bowl, mix the garlic, ginger, tamari, rice vinegar, and sugar together. Pour over the cabbage mixture and add the green onions, then mix again to combine. Just before serving, toss the kimchi with the oil and sesame seeds. The kimchi will keep well stored in an airtight container in the fridge for 2 weeks.

Note: Gochugaru, or Korean red chile flakes, is available in Asian markets or online from Amazon. com. Alternatively, you can substitute ground Aleppo chiles or *chile de árbol* powder. Gomasio mix is a Japanese ingredient and can be found in Asian markets, health food stores, or ordered online from Amazon.com.

Croque Monsieur

Makes 4 servings

· ·

What is a croque monsieur? Well, it is a humble ham and cheese sandwich that has been made over-the-top rich and decadent. But I've taken it one step further, making it with vegan bacon to add a smoky element and topping it with a cheesy vegan béchamel sauce. Slices of the Pineapple-Glazed Seitan Ham (page 38) taste great in this, too.

Sandwiches:
4 tablespoons vegan butter

8 slices sandwich bread

4 teaspoons Dijon mustard

4 slices vegan cheese

12 slices Tempeh Bacon (page 19) or Seitan Bacon (page 16)

Béchamel sauce:
2 tablespoons vegan butter

2 tablespoons unbleached all-purpose flour

1 cup plain unsweetened almond or soy milk

1/2 cup vegan shredded mozzarella

1/2 teaspoon Dijon mustard

1/8 teaspoon ground nutmeg

Sandwiches: Butter all 8 slices of bread on one side. Spread the mustard on the opposite side of all 8 slices of bread. Place 1 slice of cheese and 3 slices of bacon on half of the bread slices, mustard-side up. Top with the remaining slices of bread, mustard-side down.

Heat a large skillet over medium-high heat and add the sandwiches, in batches, and cook on both sides until golden brown. Arrange the grilled sandwiches on a rimmed baking sheet. Preheat the broiler.

Béchamel sauce: Melt the butter in a skillet over medium-high heat. Whisk in the flour until it is incorporated, then add the milk, whisking constantly for a few minutes until the sauce starts to thicken. Add the mozzarella, mustard, and nutmeg, and continue whisking until thick and smooth. Pour the béchamel evenly over all four sandwiches. Place under the broiler for about 5 minutes, until the tops of the sandwiches are browned.

Smoky Spicy Reuben-ish Sandwich
Makes 4 sandwiches

Vegans seem to love Reuben sandwiches nearly as much as they love bacon. There are plenty of vegan Reuben recipes out there, but what sets this one apart is the combination of spicy kimchi and sauerkraut and a Sriracha-spiked Thousand Island dressing. Serve this sandwich with additional pickles.

Thousand Island dressing:
1 cup vegan mayonnaise
1/2 cup finely chopped sweet pickles
1 tablespoon ketchup
1 tablespoon Sriracha
Salt and ground black pepper, to taste

Sandwiches:
8 slices rye bread, toasted
16 slices Tempeh Bacon (page 19) or Seitan Bacon (page 16)
1 cup sauerkraut, well drained
1 cup Quick and Easy Kimchi (page 117) or store-bought vegan kimchi

Dressing: Combine the mayonnaise, pickles, ketchup, Sriracha, and salt and pepper in a small bowl. Mix well and set aside.

Sandwiches: Spread each slice of bread with the Thousand Island dressing. Layer 4 of the bread slices with 4 slices of bacon, 1/4 cup sauerkraut, and 1/4 cup kimchi, and then top each sandwich with the remaining bread slices.

Note: If you don't like the spiciness of kimchi, or if it is hard to find, you can simply replace it with the same amount of sauerkraut.

BLT Hot Dogs with Bacon Remoulade
Makes 4 servings

. . . .

The first time I made this, I wondered why I didn't always put salad on top of my hot dogs. The creamy coolness of the salad contrasts so nicely with the warmth and savoriness of the hot dog and bacon. These are perfect for a summer cookout.

2 cups shredded lettuce
4 tablespoons Bacon Remoulade (page 113)
4 vegan hot dogs, grilled
4 hot dog buns, warmed
4 slices Tempeh Bacon (page 19) or Seitan Bacon (page 16)
1/2 cup halved grape or cherry tomatoes

In a medium bowl, combine the lettuce and the Bacon Remoulade, mixing well.

Place one grilled hot dog in each bun, along with a slice of the bacon. Divide the lettuce mixture and tomato halves evenly among each serving.

Photos opposite (top to bottom): Chihuahua Dogs (page 124), BLT Hot Dogs (page 122), Puck-Style Wiener Wurstchen (page 125); (repeat).

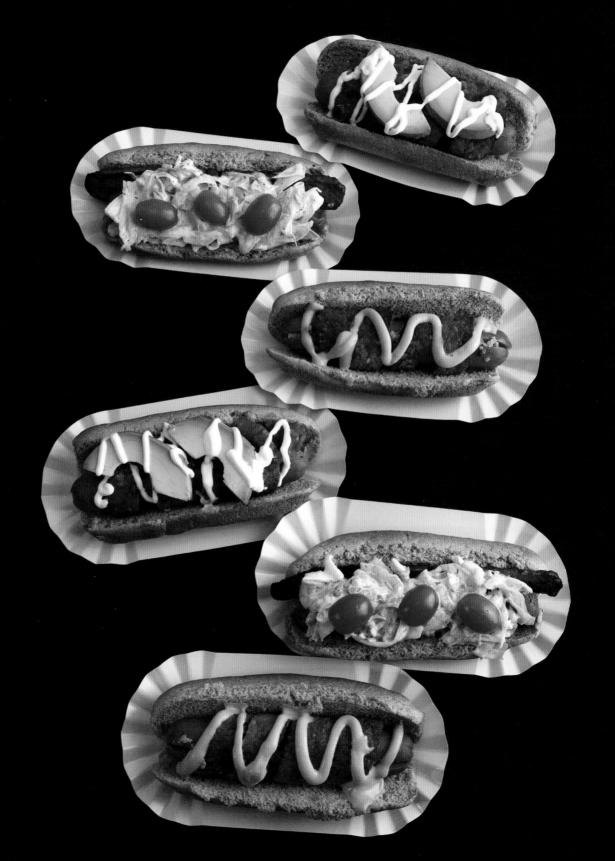

Chihuahua Dogs

Makes 6 servings

. . . .

Back before my husband and I were married, we lived in New York's East Village, near the famous Crif Dogs, a really fun late-night hot dog joint. We'd get the two-veggie-dog "Cheapskate Special" with an order of tater tots. (These dates were a lot more romantic than "Cheapskate Special" sounds). Crif Dogs are famous for a wide array of bacon-wrapped hot dogs, so this is my vegan version of their "Chihuahua," a bacon-wrapped dog topped with avocado, salsa, and sour cream. The best part is that no Chihuahuas or pigs were harmed in the making of these.

 12 slices Tempeh Bacon (page 19)
 6 vegan hot dogs
 Safflower oil, for frying
 6 whole-wheat hot dog buns, warmed
 1 ripe Hass avocado, pitted, peeled, and cut into 12 slices
 6 tablespoons hot tomato salsa
 6 tablespoons vegan sour cream
 Fresh lime wedges, for squeezing

Carefully wrap 2 slices of bacon around each hot dog, securing with toothpicks.

Add about 1/4 inch of oil to a large skillet over medium-high heat. When the oil is hot, work in batches and use tongs to carefully lower each wrapped hot dog into the oil. When you see that the bottom and sides are browned, use the tongs to carefully flip the hot dogs over, and fry on the other side until golden brown.

Remove the toothpicks and place 1 hot dog in each bun. Top each dog with 2 avocado slices, 1 tablespoon of salsa, and 1 tablespoon of sour cream. Serve with a lime wedge for squeezing.

Note: It makes it easier to flip these over and fry if all of your toothpicks are sticking out in the same direction, so that you have at least two sides of the hot dogs that are toothpick-free.

Puck-Style Wiener Wurstchen

Makes 6 servings

I came across a recipe for Wiener Wurstchen, shared by none other than Wolfgang Puck himself. These cheese-filled, bacon-wrapped hot dogs are a favorite from his childhood in Vienna. I couldn't pass up an opportunity to veganize a cheesy, bacon-wrapped hot dog and am happy to say that the results are delicious. Chef Puck serves his with a spicy horseradish sauce, but I think any spicy mustard will do. I recommend that you enjoy these with a nice, cold German beer.

  6 vegan hot dogs
  6 tablespoons vegan shredded cheese (any variety)
  12 slices Tempeh Bacon (page 19)
  Safflower oil, for frying
  6 whole-wheat hot dog buns, warmed
  Spicy mustard, for serving

Use a sharp paring knife to split each hot dog lengthwise, cutting about halfway through. Sprinkle 1 tablespoon of cheese into the center of each hot dog, then very carefully wrap 2 slices of bacon around each hot dog, securing with toothpicks. The bacon slices should mostly cover the cheese, so that it doesn't fall out during cooking.

Add about 1/4 inch of oil to a large skillet over medium-high heat. When the oil is hot, work in batches and use tongs to carefully lower each wrapped hot dog into the oil. When you see that the bottom and sides are browned, use the tongs to carefully flip the hot dogs over, and fry on the other side until golden brown. Remove the toothpicks and place 1 hot dog in each bun. Serve with mustard.

Note: It's easier to flip these over and fry if all of the toothpicks are sticking out in the same direction, so that you have at least two sides of the hot dogs that are toothpick-free.

Asian-Style Vegetables with Bacon (page 137)

Sides

· ·

It's easy to eat all your veggies when you have side dishes as tasty and as loaded with baconish flavor as these. Brussels sprouts, cauliflower, asparagus, beans—they all benefit from some extra salty, smoky savoriness. Whether you wrap your veggies with strips of Tempeh Bacon or sprinkle some vegan bacon on top of the finished dish, you're going to love eating your vegetables even more when they taste baconish.

Brussels Sprouts with Bacon and Shallots

Makes 4 to 6 servings

Shallots and vegan bacon are caramelized with a bit of brown sugar to add just a touch of sweetness to the earthiness of the Brussels sprouts in this recipe. I prefer my Brussels on the crisp-crunchy side, but feel free to cook them longer if you like them more well done.

- 3 tablespoons olive oil, divided
- 6 large shallots, sliced paper thin
- 5 to 6 slices Tofu Bacon (page 18), Tempeh Bacon (page 19), or Seitan Bacon (page 16), chopped
- 1 tablespoon brown sugar
- 1 1/2 pounds Brussels sprouts, stems trimmed, halved (quartered if very large)
- 1/3 cup dry white wine

Heat 1 tablespoon of the oil in a medium skillet over medium-high heat. Add the shallots and bacon and cook for 3 to 4 minutes, stirring, until the shallots are translucent. Sprinkle with the brown sugar and continue cooking until the shallots are browned and caramelized. Set aside.

Heat the remaining 2 tablespoons of oil in a large skillet over medium-high heat. Add the Brussels sprouts to the pan in a single layer, cut-side down. Leave undisturbed 2 to 3 minutes before stirring, to help them brown and caramelize. Continue to cook and stir occasionally until the Brussels sprouts turn bright green.

Add the white wine to the Brussels sprouts, cover immediately, and steam for 2 minutes. Uncover and cook until all the liquid has evaporated and the Brussels sprouts are tender, about 6 to 8 minutes. Stir in the shallot-bacon mixture and serve hot.

Cauliflower Bacon Gratin

Makes 4 to 6 servings

. . . .

It wasn't until well into adulthood that I discovered the sweet nuttiness of this underrated crucifer-ous treat. Cauliflower can really shine, as it does in this incredibly comforting, creamy dish.

Cauliflower:

1 medium head cauliflower, chopped into small florets

1 tablespoon olive oil

1 medium onion, finely chopped

2 cloves garlic, finely chopped

1 cup raw cashews

1 cup plain unsweetened almond or soy milk

3 tablespoons nutritional yeast

1 tablespoon cornstarch

1 teaspoon Dijon mustard

8 slices Seitan Bacon (page 16), chopped into 1/2-inch pieces

Salt and ground black pepper, to taste

Topping:

1/2 cup dried breadcrumbs

1 tablespoon olive oil

1/3 cup vegan shredded cheese (any variety) or vegan Parmesan sprinkles

Preheat the oven to 350°F. Lightly grease an 8 x 8-inch baking pan. Bring about 1 quart of water to a boil in a medium saucepan. Add the cauliflower, cook 2 minutes, then drain. Transfer the cauliflower to a large mixing bowl and set aside.

Heat the oil in a medium skillet over medium heat. Add the onion and garlic and cook for 5 minutes, stirring occasionally, until the onion is soft and translucent.

In a blender, combine the cashews, milk, nutritional yeast, cornstarch, mustard, and onion and gar-lic (with any oil left in the skillet) and blend until smooth. Pour the mixture over the cauliflower, fold in the bacon, and toss so that everything is coated evenly. Season with salt and pepper to taste.

In a small bowl, mix the breadcrumbs and oil with your fingers. The crumbs should be moist, but not wet. Mix in the cheese. Distribute the crumb mixture evenly over the cauliflower and bake for 35 minutes, or until the top of the gratin is golden brown.

Bacon-Wrapped Asparagus

Makes 9 bundles

Asparagus bundles wrapped in bacon and drizzled with a soy-sesame sauce make a perfect side dish for any time of year. I use Tempeh Bacon for this, because it's the most flexible and easiest to wrap around the asparagus.

1 tablespoon olive oil

36 asparagus spears, tough ends trimmed

Salt and ground black pepper, to taste

9 slices Tempeh Bacon (page 19), uncooked

2 tablespoons tamari

2 tablespoons brown sugar

2 cloves garlic, minced

1 tablespoon sesame oil

1 tablespoon vegan butter

2 teaspoons sesame seeds

Preheat the oven to 400°F. Line a large rimmed baking pan with foil.

Drizzle the olive oil over the asparagus, just enough to barely coat the stalks, then season with salt and pepper to taste.

Divide the asparagus into bundles of four. Wrap one Tempeh Bacon strip around each bundle and secure with a toothpick if necessary. Place the bundles on the prepared baking sheet.

In a small saucepan over low heat, whisk together the tamari, brown sugar, garlic, sesame oil, and butter. Heat just until the butter and sugar are melted. Drizzle the sauce evenly over the asparagus bundles. Sprinkle with the sesame seeds.

Bake the bundles for 25 minutes, or until the asparagus is cooked through. Use a large spatula to lift the bundles off the baking sheet to serve.

Smoky Barbecue-Bacon Baked Beans

Makes 8 to 10 servings

. . . .

I love baked beans. My dad still makes them for pretty much any family gathering that we have, and I feel like summer barbecues are incomplete without them. This recipe hits just the right balance of smoky, sweet, and savory.

- 1 tablespoon olive oil
- 1 small onion, finely chopped
- 2 cloves garlic, finely chopped
- 1 cup chopped Tempeh Bacon (page 19) plus 6 additional slices for topping
- 2 (15-ounce) cans navy beans, rinsed and drained
- 1 cup barbecue sauce
- 1 teaspoon liquid smoke (optional, but recommended)
- 1/4 cup brown sugar
- 1/2 cup maple syrup
- 2 tablespoons ketchup
- 2 tablespoons Dijon mustard
- 4 sprigs fresh thyme

Preheat the oven to 350°F. Heat the oil in a large deep-sided cast iron skillet over medium-high heat. Add the onion, garlic, and chopped Tempeh Bacon and cook, stirring occasionally, for 6 to 8 minutes, or until the onion is translucent and the bacon is browned all over. Add the navy beans, barbecue sauce, liquid smoke, brown sugar, maple syrup, ketchup, mustard, and thyme. Mix thoroughly so that the beans are evenly coated. Arrange the Tempeh Bacon slices on top of the beans.

Bake the beans for 50 minutes, or until thick and bubbly, so that there is little liquid left and the Tempeh Bacon is browned on the top.

Note: If you don't have a cast iron skillet, sauté the onion, garlic, and bacon in a regular skillet, then transfer to a casserole dish before adding all the other ingredients.

Asian-Style Vegetables with Bacon

Makes 6 to 8 servings

This is a go-to recipe for stir-fried vegetables that works well with any of the vegan bacons. It is super easy and quick to make.

3 tablespoons tamari

3 tablespoons agave nectar

2 teaspoons rice wine vinegar

2 teaspoons Sriracha or other chili sauce

1 teaspoon cornstarch

2 tablespoons dark sesame oil

2 pounds green beans, broccoli, or bok choy (or a combination), cut into
   bite-size pieces

2 cloves garlic, minced

1 tablespoon minced fresh ginger

1 cup chopped and cooked King Trumpet Mushroom Bacon (page 25 or other vegan bacon

In a small bowl, combine the tamari, agave, rice wine vinegar, Sriracha, and cornstarch, and whisk to blend. Set aside.

Heat the oil in a wok or large deep-sided nonstick skillet over medium-high heat. Add the green beans, broccoli, and/or bok choy and stir-fry for 4 to 5 minutes. Add the garlic and ginger, and stir-fry for 1 minute. Add the sauce and stir-fry for 1 minute (the sauce will thicken quickly). Stir quickly to coat all the vegetables. When the vegetables are coated and done to your liking, add the bacon and toss to combine. Serve hot.

Bacon Fried Rice

Makes 4 servings

. . . .

We eat a lot of rice in my home, and I always make an extra-large pot of it in order to have plenty left over for fried rice the next day. I love to use Tofu Bacon in this, because I love tofu in my fried rice anyway, but any of the vegan bacons work well here.

    4 tablespoons safflower oil, divided
    1 cup chopped Tofu Bacon (page 18)
    4 cloves garlic, smashed and finely chopped
    4 green onions, white and green parts, thinly sliced (reserve some green
        parts for garnish)
    1 tablespoon grated fresh ginger
    1 cup snow peas, tough strings removed and cut in half diagonally
    1 cup frozen peas and carrots, thawed
    4 cups leftover cooked rice (white or brown), chilled
    3 tablespoons tamari
    2 tablespoons dark sesame oil
    Ground black pepper, to taste
    Chili sauce, for serving

Heat 1 tablespoon of the safflower oil in a wok or large, deep-sided skillet over medium-high heat. Add the Tofu Bacon and stir-fry until browned, 4 to 5 minutes. Remove from the wok and set aside.

Turn the heat up to high. Add the 3 remaining tablespoons of safflower oil. When the oil is shimmering, add the garlic, green onions, and ginger. Stir-fry 1 to 2 minutes or until the onions and garlic are softened. Add the snow peas and peas and carrots. Stir-fry for 3 minutes, or until the vegetables are heated through. Add the rice, stirring to combine and break up any lumps. Drizzle the tamari and sesame oil over the rice. Continue to stir-fry until everything is cooked through, 4 to 5 minutes. Stir in the bacon, then season with a generous amount of pepper. Serve with chili sauce.

Mains

• •

Creamy, luscious pasta carbonara. Salty, sweet Hawaiian pizza. Elegant, savory Alsatian onion tart. Hearty, mushroom-filled buckwheat
crepes. A scrumptious white wine risotto dotted with peas. Crispy, pil-
lowy potato pierogi. Protein-packed, all-American veggie loaf. And the
richest, creamiest smoky mac and cheese. What do all of these things
have in common? Vegan bacon! Smoky, savory baconish flavor takes
all of the main dishes in this chapter to the next level of deliciousness.
As a topping on your pizza or sprinkled atop your pasta, any way you
use it, everything really is better with vegan bacon.

Tofu Bacon Carbonara

Makes 6 to 8 servings

. . . .

Traditional carbonara sauce includes eggs, cheese, and bacon. It is a heart attack on a plate! This carbonara is lightened up and heart-healthy, but still incredibly rich and comforting.

    16 ounces linguine or fettuccine
    3 tablespoons olive oil, divided
    6 ounces Tofu Bacon (page 18), chopped
    1 medium onion, finely chopped
    2 cloves garlic, finely chopped
    2 cups raw cashews
    3/4 cup plain unsweetened almond milk
    3/4 cup vegetable broth
    1/4 cup nutritional yeast
    1/4 cup vegan Parmesan, plus more for serving
    1/2 teaspoon salt
    Ground black pepper, to taste
    2 tablespoons chopped fresh parsley, for garnish

Bring 4 quarts of salted water to a boil in a large pot. Add the pasta boil for 7 to 10 minutes, or until al dente. Drain and return the pasta to the pot, reserving 1 cup of the cooking water.

Heat 1 tablespoon of the oil in a skillet over medium-high heat. Add the Tofu Bacon and cook for 4 to 5 minutes, until browned on both sides. Remove the bacon from the skillet and chop it into 1/4-inch pieces. Heat the remaining 2 tablespoons of oil in the same skillet over medium heat. Add the onion and cook for about 4 minutes, or until softened, then add the garlic and cook another minute. Remove from the heat.

Grind the cashews in a blender, pulsing until they are powdery. Add the onion, garlic, milk, broth, nutritional yeast, and Parmesan. Blend until smooth. Add the sauce, bacon, salt, and pepper to the cooked pasta, and toss over low heat to combine until heated through. If the sauce seems too thick, or thickens upon standing, add some of the reserved pasta cooking water until it reaches the desired consistency. Garnish with fresh parsley and additional vegan Parmesan, if desired. Serve immediately.

Butternut Squash Carbonara

with BACON AND SAGE

Makes 4 servings

. . . .

The sauce in this recipe is luscious and silky smooth, a wonderful and healthy interpretation of a traditional carbonara, which is loaded with cream and egg yolks. It's so good you may want to lick the plate clean.

    2 tablespoons olive oil
    6 slices Tempeh Bacon (page 19) or other vegan bacon, finely chopped
    2 tablespoons finely chopped fresh sage
    2 pounds butternut squash or kabocha squash, peeled, seeded, and cut
        into 1/2-inch pieces
    1 small onion, coarsely chopped
    2 cloves garlic, coarsely chopped
    Salt and ground black pepper, to taste
    2 cups vegetable broth
    12 ounces fettucine or linguine

Heat the oil in a large skillet over medium-high heat. Add the bacon and cook until crisp and browned, stirring occasionally, about 5 minutes. Add the sage and toss to coat. Transfer the bacon and sage to a small bowl and set aside.

Add the squash, onion, and garlic to the same skillet over medium heat. Season with salt and pepper and cook, stirring occasionally, until onion is translucent, 8 to 10 minutes. Add the broth and bring to a boil. Reduce to a simmer and cook until the squash is soft and the liquid is reduced by half, 15 to 20 minutes. Let the squash mixture cool for a few minutes then transfer it to a blender and puree until smooth. Set aside and reserve the skillet.

Cook the pasta in a large pot of salted boiling water. Drain, reserving 1 cup of the cooking water.

Combine the pasta, pureed squash, and about 1/4 cup of the cooking water in the skillet. Toss and cook over medium heat, until the pasta is thoroughly coated. If the sauce is too thick, add more of the pasta cooking water as needed. Serve the pasta topped with the Tempeh Bacon and sage.

Pasta with Leeks and Bacon
Makes 4 to 6 servings

The delicate sweetness of leeks pairs wonderfully with savory bacon and a light creamy sauce in this simple but delicious pasta.

16 ounces fettucine, spaghetti, or linguini

2 tablespoons olive oil

6 ounces (about 1 heaping cup) chopped Tempeh Bacon (page 19), Seitan Bacon (page 16), or Tofu Bacon (page 18)

2 leeks, halved lengthwise, white and pale green parts cut into 1/4-inch slices

4 ounces vegan sour cream or cream cheese

1/2 cup vegan Parmesan

1 teaspoon dried thyme

Salt and ground black pepper, to taste

Bring 5 quarts of salted water to a boil in a large pot. Add the pasta and cook 8 to 10 minutes, or until al dente. Drain the pasta, reserving 1 1/2 cups of the cooking water.

Heat the oil in a large skillet over medium heat. Add the bacon and cook for 2 to 3 minutes. Add the leeks and cook for about 5 minutes, or until the leeks start to brown. Stir in the sour cream, Parmesan, thyme, and 3/4 cup of the cooking water. When the sauce is well blended, add the drained pasta and use tongs to toss and coat it evenly. If the sauce is too thick, or thickens upon standing, add additional cooking water. Season with salt and pepper.

Pasta with Zucchini, Corn, and Bacon

Makes 4 servings

. . . .

This is a very easy pasta dish to throw together and has the wonderful summer flavors of fresh corn, zucchini, and fresh basil. Any of the bacons are great in this recipe.

- 8 ounces pasta (any kind)
- 3 tablespoons olive oil
- 1 large zucchini (about 1 pound), cut lengthwise then into 1/4-inch half-moon slices
- 2 ears corn, kernels removed (about 1 1/2 cups; thawed frozen corn is fine, too)
- 3 cloves garlic, minced
- 1 cup chopped vegan bacon (any kind)
- 1/2 cup fresh torn basil leaves
- Salt and ground black pepper, to taste

Cook the pasta in a large pot of boiling salted water until it is al dente. While the pasta is cooking, heat the oil in a large, deep-sided skillet over medium-high heat. Add the zucchini, corn, garlic, and bacon until everything is browned and the zucchini is tender.

Drain the pasta, reserving 1/2 cup of the pasta water. Add the pasta to the pan, using tongs to toss the ingredients together. Add the pasta water, 2 tablespoons at a time, to moisten the pasta (you may not need the entire amount of water). Add the torn basil leaves and season with salt and pepper to taste.

Spinach and Bacon Stuffed Shells
Makes 4 to 6 servings

I love to make stuffed shells whenever we have company for dinner, because they're easy to assemble ahead of time and just pop in the oven when it's time for dinner. These baked shells are luscious and creamy, with just a hint of smokiness.

18 jumbo pasta shells
2 tablespoons olive oil
1 medium onion, finely chopped
1 cup finely chopped Tempeh Bacon (page 19) or your favorite vegan bacon
2 cloves garlic, minced
5 ounces baby spinach
16 ounces firm tofu, drained
1 cup vegan mayonnaise
1 (25-ounce) jar marinara sauce
2 to 3 tablespoons vegan Parmesan

Preheat the oven to 350°F. Lightly spray a 9 x 13-inch baking dish with nonstick cooking spray.

Bring 3 quarts of water to a boil, then add the pasta shells. Cook the shells for 8 to 10 minutes, until just al dente, then drain and set aside.

Heat the oil in a large nonstick skillet over medium-high heat. Add the onion and bacon and cook for 4 to 5 minutes, or until the onion is softened and translucent and the bacon is beginning to brown. Add the garlic, and cook another minute. Add the spinach and cook another 1 to 2 minutes, until the leaves are just wilted. Remove from the heat and set aside.

Crumble the tofu into a food processor. Add the mayonnaise and pulse 3 to 4 times, until well combined. Add the spinach and onion mixture, then pulse about 10 times. (You don't need the filling to be super smooth, you just want the spinach to be finely minced.)

Spread a thin layer of marinara sauce on the bottom of the baking dish. Stuff each shell with 2 rounded tablespoons of the filling, then arrange them in the dish. Pour the remaining sauce over the top of the shells, and sprinkle with the vegan Parmesan. Bake for 30 minutes. Serve hot.

BLT Pasta

Makes 4 servings

· ·

This quick and easy pasta is great to make with any of the vegan bacons. If you are using Tofu, Tempeh, or Seitan Bacon, pan-fry the slices in a little olive oil before adding to the pasta. If using any of the other vegan bacons, simply toss them in just before serving.

 8 ounces pasta (any kind)
2 tablespoons olive oil, divided
2 cups cherry tomatoes, halved
5 ounces baby spinach
1 1/2 cups chopped vegan bacon (any kind; see headnote)
Salt and ground black pepper, to taste

Bring 1 quart of salted water to a boil. Add the pasta and boil for 8 to 10 minutes, until al dente. Drain and set aside.

Heat 1 tablespoon of the oil in a large, deep-sided skillet. Add the tomatoes and cook for 2 minutes. Add the spinach and cook another minute, until the spinach is just barely wilted. Add the cooked pasta to the skillet with the remaining 1 tablespoon of oil, using tongs to toss the mixture together. Add the bacon, then season with salt and pepper to taste. Serve hot.

BLT Pizza
Makes 4 to 6 servings

This is a super fast and easy pizza recipe that you can throw together in minutes. It's almost as easy as ordering delivery, but so much healthier and tastier. Plus, you're having fresh greens on the pizza, so it's basically like eating a salad. Right? (See photo on page 140.)

  1 Quick and Easy Whole-Wheat Pizza Crust (page 155) or store-bought
     crust (see note), at room temperature
  2/3 cup store-bought pizza sauce
  3/4 cup vegan shredded mozzarella cheese
  1/3 cup chopped Tofu Bacon (page 18), marinated but not cooked
  1/2 cup cherry tomatoes, halved
  1 cup arugula leaves

Preheat the oven to 475°F.

Stretch the pizza crust dough onto a 12-inch round pizza pan. Spread the pizza sauce evenly over the crust to within 1 inch of the edge. Sprinkle the mozzarella evenly on top of the sauce. Distribute the Tofu Bacon pieces and cherry tomatoes over the mozzarella.

Bake the pizza for 12 to 15 minutes, or until the cheese is completely melted and the Tofu Bacon is browned. Remove the pizza from the oven, arrange the arugula leaves all over the top, cut into slices, and serve.

Note: Look for whole-wheat pizza dough at Whole Foods, Trader Joe's, and natural food stores.

Quick and Easy Whole-Wheat Pizza Crust
Makes 2 (12-inch) pizza crusts

. . . .

This pizza crust takes only a few minutes to make, without all that time for dough rising. This recipe makes two thin but hearty whole-wheat crusts. For a super thin, cracker-like crust, use just 1/4 to 1/3 of the recipe.

1 cup hot water (about 110°F)
1 (1/4-ounce) packet rapid-rise yeast
1 tablespoon sugar
1 tablespoon olive oil, plus more for brushing
2 1/2 cups whole-wheat flour
2 tablespoons vegan Parmesan
1 teaspoon salt
1 teaspoon dried oregano
1 teaspoon dried basil

In a small bowl, combine the hot water, yeast, sugar, and oil and let stand for 5 minutes, until frothy.

In a food processor, combine the flour, Parmesan, salt, oregano, and basil, and pulse to mix. With the processor running, slowly pour in the yeast mixture and mix until the dough forms a loose ball.

Transfer the dough onto a floured work surface and knead it a few times, until it holds together in a ball. Divide the dough in half.

Roll each half out into a 12-inch circle. Transfer to a pizza pan or baking sheet. Lightly brush oil around the outer inch of crust. Your crust is now ready to top and bake.

Hawaiian Pizza

Makes 4 to 6 servings

For the longest time, I refused on principle to even try Hawaiian pizza. Pineapple on pizza sounded crazy to me. When I finally realized that I'm all about sweet and savory combinations, I gave it a try, and now I'm hooked. I think you will be, too.

- 1 Quick and Easy Whole-Wheat Pizza Crust (page 155) or store-bought crust (see note), at room temperature
- 2/3 cup store-bought pizza sauce
- 1/2 to 1 cup vegan shredded mozzarella cheese (depending on how cheesy you like it)
- 1/2 cup chopped Tofu Bacon (page 18), marinated but not cooked
- 3/4 cup chopped fresh pineapple
- 1/4 large red onion, sliced paper thin
- 1/3 cup loosely packed fresh cilantro leaves, for serving

Preheat the oven to 475°F.

Place the pizza crust on a 12-inch round pizza pan. Spread the pizza sauce evenly over the crust to within 1 inch of the edge. Sprinkle the mozzarella shreds evenly on top of the sauce, then arrange the Tofu Bacon, pineapple, and red onion evenly over the mozzarella.

Bake the pizza for 12 to 15 minutes, then remove from the oven, top with cilantro, and cut into slices. Serve hot.

Note: Look for whole-wheat pizza dough at Whole Foods, Trader Joe's, and natural food stores.

Flammkuchen

(ALSATIAN BACON and ONION TART)
Makes 4 servings

. . . .

Also referred to as *tarte flambée* in French, this treat hails from the Alsace region of France, bordering Germany. I have family that lives not far from there, and it is one of my favorite regions to visit. This tart is traditionally covered in crème fraîche, thinly sliced onions, and bacon lardons. To make it the most authentic, use as thin a crust as possible, so that it is very crispy and nearly cracker-like.

- 1 Quick and Easy Whole-Wheat Pizza Crust (page 155) or store-bought crust (see note), at room temperature
- 4 ounces vegan cream cheese, softened
- 1/4 cup vegan shredded mozzarella cheese
- 1 teaspoon lemon juice
- 1/2 teaspoon dried thyme
- 1 small white or yellow onion, sliced paper thin
- 1/2 cup Tofu Bacon lardons (page 18)
- 4 teaspoons chopped fresh chives, for serving

Preheat the oven to 550°F or the highest setting. If you have a pizza stone, place it in the oven to heat. If you don't have one, place a large baking sheet upside down in the oven while it heats (this will make it easier to slide the tart on and off the pizza peel). Cut the pizza crust dough in half and reserve one half for another use. Roll out the remaining pizza crust dough until it is very thin.

In a medium bowl, combine the vegan cream cheese, mozzarella, lemon juice, and thyme. Spread this mixture evenly on the pizza dough, all the way to the edges. There is no need to leave a border around the crust.

Distribute the onion slices and lardons evenly over the surface of the crust. Use a pizza peel to place the tart in the oven. (If you don't have a pizza peel, I recommend building the tart on parchment paper, leaving about 1 inch of parchment border around the tart, then using either a rimless baking sheet or an upside-down rimmed baking sheet to transfer it to the oven.) Bake the tart for 10 minutes, until golden brown and crispy. Remove it from the oven, then garnish it with chopped fresh chives.

Note: Look for whole-wheat pizza dough at Whole Foods, Trader Joe's, and natural food stores.

Bacon and Butternut Squash Galette

Makes 4 to 6 servings

Butternut squash is another vegetable that pairs beautifully with bacon, the earthy sweetness contrasting with the salty savoriness. This is a very simple and rustic tart that is perfect for the fall or on any holiday table.

- 1 1/4 pounds butternut squash, peeled, seeded, and cut into 1-inch cubes
- 3 tablespoons olive oil, divided
- 1/4 teaspoon salt
- 1 medium onion, coarsely chopped
- 2 cloves garlic, minced
- 1/2 teaspoon dried sage
- 1 teaspoon dried thyme
- 1 cup chopped Tempeh Bacon (page 19) or Seitan Bacon (page 16)
- 1 Quick and Easy Whole-Wheat Pizza Crust (page 155) or store-bought crust

Preheat the oven to 450°F. Line a large rimmed baking sheet with parchment paper.

Arrange the butternut squash cubes in an even layer on the prepared baking sheet. Drizzle with 1 tablespoon of the oil and the salt. Roast the squash for about 15 minutes, or until the cubes begin to brown around the edges. Remove the squash from the oven, then lower the heat to 350°F.

While the squash is baking, heat the remaining 2 tablespoons of oil in a medium skillet over medium-high heat. Add the onion, garlic, and bacon, and cook for 5 minutes, stirring occasionally, until the onion is soft and beginning to brown. Add the sage and thyme, and cook 1 minute longer.

Roll out the pizza crust into a circle and arrange it on the baking sheet. Arrange the squash evenly over the crust, to within about 1 inch from the edges. Arrange the bacon and onion mixture over the squash cubes. Fold the crust edges inward, all around. Bake the galette for 30 to 35 minutes, or until the crust is golden brown.

Risotto with Peas and Mushroom Bacon

Makes 6 servings

It seems that in every food show I've ever seen with Gordon Ramsey, he yells at someone about messing up their risotto. Despite its reputation, risotto is actually not that difficult to make. It does help to imagine the voice of Gordon Ramsey in your head while you're making it, just to keep yourself in line.

6 cups vegetable broth
2 tablespoons olive oil
1 medium onion, finely chopped
12 ounces shiitake mushrooms, stemmed and sliced
2 cloves garlic, minced
1/2 teaspoon dried rosemary
1/2 cup dry white wine
2 cups Arborio rice
3/4 cup frozen peas
2 tablespoons vegan Parmesan, optional
Salt and ground black pepper, to taste
1/3 cup Shiitake Mushroom Bacon (page 26), for serving

Bring the broth to a simmer in a medium saucepan over high heat, then keep it warm over low heat.

Heat the oil in a large nonstick skillet over medium heat. Add the onion and cook 2 minutes. Add the mushrooms and cook for 4 minutes. Add the garlic and rosemary and cook another minute. Add the wine and cook, stirring for 1 minute, until the liquid is mostly absorbed. Add the rice and cook for 1 minute, stirring to coat the rice.

Begin adding the hot broth, 1/2 cup at a time, stirring constantly until it is absorbed before adding another 1/2 cup. It will take approximately 20 to 25 minutes until all the broth is added this way.

Stir in the peas and cook another 3 to 4 minutes, or until the peas are warmed through. Stir in the Parmesan, if using. Season with salt and pepper to taste. Divide the risotto evenly among six shallow bowls and top each serving with the Shiitake Bacon. Serve hot.

Potato, Bacon, and Onion Pierogi
Makes 8 servings

· ·

When I was in school in Paris, I spent one spring break at the home of a dear Polish friend. We had a great time exploring the beautiful cities of Warsaw and Krakow, but one of the highlights of the trip was her mom's homemade pierogi. I think of that trip and the wonderful hospitality every time I eat these delicious, savory dumplings. They are a lot of work, but they are worth it. (See photo on page 166.)

Dough:

1/4 cup safflower oil

3 tablespoons aquafaba (page 8)

1 teaspoon salt

3 1/4 cups unbleached all-purpose flour, plus more for kneading

1 cup water

Filling:

3 medium russet potatoes (about 1 1/4 pounds)

1 tablespoon olive oil

3/4 cup minced onion

2 tablespoons plain unsweetened almond or soy milk

1/3 cup vegan shredded cheddar cheese

1/2 teaspoon dried thyme

1/2 teaspoon salt

1/2 teaspoon ground black pepper

1/3 cup Baconish Bits (page 32)

Vegan butter, for frying

Vegan sour cream, for serving

Chopped fresh chives, for serving

Dough: Combine the safflower oil, aquafaba, and salt in a large bowl and mix well. Mix in about 1 cup flour, then 1/4 cup water, alternating until it is all well combined.

Transfer the dough to a floured work surface and knead until you have a smooth ball, 5 to 6 minutes. It should be very soft and not too sticky. If it is sticking to your hands, sprinkle more flour on it until you can work with it without sticking. Wrap the dough in plastic and refrigerate for 1 hour.

Filling: Peel the potatoes and cut them into 1-inch pieces. Transfer the potato pieces to a large pot and cover with cold water. Bring to a boil and cook for 10 minutes or until very soft and easily pierced with a fork. Drain the potatoes and return them to the pot.

While the potatoes are boiling, heat the olive oil in a medium skillet over medium heat. Add the onion and cook 4 to 5 minutes, stirring only occasionally, until lightly browned.

Mash the cooked potatoes with the milk and cheddar. Add the thyme, salt, and pepper, then fold in the onion and Baconish Bits. Mix until well combined.

Line 2 large baking sheets with parchment paper. Divide the dough in half, then rewrap one half and return it to the refrigerator until ready to use. Place the half you are working with on a floured surface and roll to a 1/8-inch thickness. Use a 3-inch round biscuit or cookie cutter to cut out rounds. Place 1 rounded teaspoon of filling just off the center of each round. Fold the wider half over the top of the filling and pinch closed with your fingers to seal the edges. (I find it is easiest to pinch the edge together first in the middle, and then around the sides. This dough is very forgiving and easy to work with, as long as you keep all surfaces floured, including your fingertips.) Place the sealed pierogi on the prepared baking sheets until ready to cook.

Bring a large pot of water to a boil. Add about 12 pierogi at a time to the boiling water, working in batches so as to not overcrowd them. Cook until the pierogi float to the surface, then boil about 5 minutes longer.

Heat 1 tablespoon of butter in a large nonstick skillet over medium-high heat. When the pierogi are done boiling, remove them with a slotted spoon and transfer them to the already hot skillet. Fry on both sides for 2 to 3 minutes, until golden brown and crispy. Serve with vegan sour cream and chopped fresh chives.

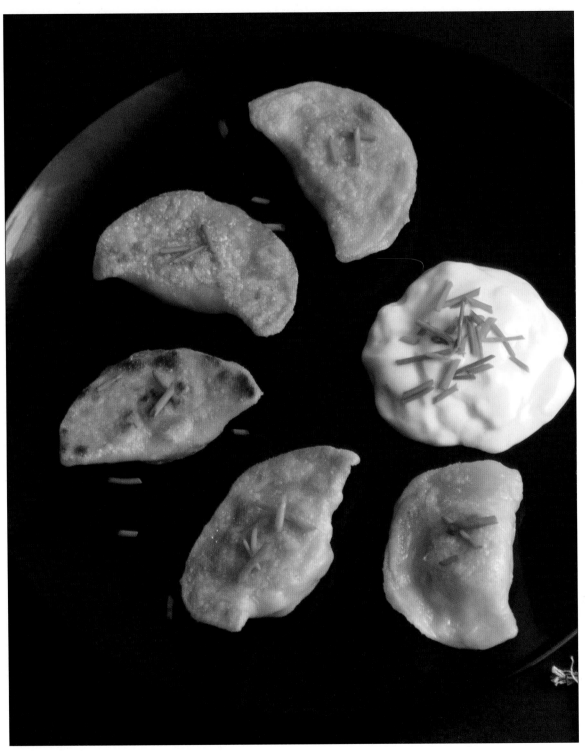

Potato, Bacon, and Onion Pierogi (page 164)

Buckwheat Crepes with Mushrooms and Bacon (page 168)

Buckwheat Crepes

with MUSHROOMS and BACON

Makes 6 servings

. . . .

When I lived in Paris, I loved to get the savory crêpes au sarrasin for lunch, which is the French name for these Breton-style buckwheat crepes. They are heartier and darker than the thin, sweet crepe that most people are familiar with. These are wonderful for lunch or dinner with a glass of wine. (See photo on previous page.)

Crepes:

1/2 cup unbleached all-purpose flour

1/2 cup buckwheat flour

1/2 teaspoon salt

1/2 teaspoon ground black pepper

1/4 teaspoon sugar

1 3/4 cup plain unsweetened almond milk

3 tablespoons aquafaba (page 8) or egg replacer of your choice equivalent to one egg (page 13)

3 to 4 tablespoons vegan butter

Filling:

3 tablespoons vegan butter, divided

1/2 cup chopped Tempeh Bacon (page 19), Seitan Bacon (page 16), or Tofu Bacon (page 18)

8 ounces button, porcini, shiitake, or wild mushrooms, cleaned and cut into 1/8-inch slices

1/4 cup unbleached all-purpose flour

1 1/2 cups plain unsweetened almond milk

2 tablespoons vegan shredded mozzarella cheese

2 tablespoons chopped fresh parsley

1/4 teaspoon lemon juice

Salt and ground black pepper, to taste

Preheat the oven to 200°F.

Crepes: Combine the all-purpose flour, buckwheat flour, salt, pepper, and sugar in a large bowl.

Whisk in the milk and aquafaba until smooth. Melt 1 tablespoon of the butter in a medium nonstick skillet over medium heat. Use a 1/2-cup measure to scoop the crepe batter into the pan, then immediately swirl the pan gently so the batter spreads out into as thin a circle as possible, about 7 inches across. Cook 2 to 3 minutes until it looks mostly dry, then with a very wide, thin spatula carefully flip the crepe over to cook another minute on the other side. Remove from the pan and keep the crepes stacked in the oven on a baking sheet while you cook the rest of the batter. Add small amounts of butter to the pan as necessary if it gets too dry. You should end up with a total of 6 crepes.

Filling: Melt 1 tablespoon of the butter in a medium skillet over medium heat. Add the bacon and mushrooms and cook for about 5 minutes, until browned, then remove the mixture from the skillet and set aside.

Melt the remaining 2 tablespoons of butter in the same skillet. Whisk in the flour quickly so that you have a smooth paste. Add the milk, whisking constantly to avoid any lumps. Add the mozzarella, parsley, and lemon juice, then season with salt and pepper to taste. Mix in the bacon and mushroom mixture. If the sauce begins to get too thick, add small amounts of milk until it is the consistency you like.

To serve, place each crepe on a plate. Divide the filling evenly among the 6 crepes, spooning the filling down the center of each crepe, then fold each side over. Serve immediately.

Bacon-Topped Veggie Loaf
Makes 6 to 8 servings

. . . .

This might look like a long list of ingredients, but using a food processor to blend everything up makes this recipe a snap to make. I tried many different versions of this before I finally landed upon a recipe that makes a moist, firm meatless loaf that doesn't fall apart. Pan-fry leftover slices for an excellent "meatloaf" sandwich the next day.

1 medium onion, chopped into large chunks

1 large carrot, cut into large chunks

2 tablespoons olive oil

8 ounces button mushrooms, cleaned and stems trimmed

1 (15-ounce) can lentils, rinsed and drained, divided

1 cup cooked brown rice

2 cloves garlic, halved

3 tablespoons tamari

2 tablespoons tomato paste

1 tablespoon Dijon mustard

1 tablespoon vegan Worcestershire sauce

1 tablespoon dried parsley

1/2 teaspoon dried sage

1/2 teaspoon dried rosemary

1/2 teaspoon salt

1/2 teaspoon ground black pepper

1/4 cup Baconish Bits (page 32)

1/2 cup cornmeal

5 to 6 slices Tempeh Bacon (page 19)

1/4 cup barbecue sauce

Preheat the oven to 375°F. Line a 9 x 5-inch loaf pan with aluminum foil, leaving several inches of overhang on both sides. Lightly spray foil with nonstick cooking spray.

Place the onion and carrot chunks into a food processor and pulse about 10 times until they are coarsely chopped.

Heat the oil in a large skillet over medium heat. Add the onion and carrot and cook for about 6 minutes, or until the onion is soft and translucent. While the onion and carrot are cooking, add the mushrooms to the food processor and pulse about 5 times. Add the mushrooms to the onion and carrot mixture, and cook about 5 more minutes. Remove from the heat and transfer to a large mixing bowl.

Add 1 cup of the lentils to the food processor, along with the rice, garlic, tamari, tomato paste, mustard, vegan Worcestershire, parsley, sage, rosemary, salt, and pepper. Process until well combined, but not pureed. It should still have a bit of texture.

Transfer the mixture to the bowl containing the carrots and mushrooms. Fold in the remaining 1/2 cup whole lentils, Baconish Bits, and cornmeal. Mix until well combined.

Spread the mixture evenly into the prepared loaf pan and smooth the top with a spatula. Arrange the bacon slices on top of the loaf, then spread the barbecue sauce over them and smooth with a spatula.

Cover the loaf with foil and bake for 30 minutes. Uncover and bake an additional 15 minutes. Allow the loaf to cool at least 15 minutes before slicing and serving. If you want to serve it out of the pan, the loaf will lift out easily using the foil flaps that you left hanging over the edge of the pan.

Smoky Bacon Mac and Cheese
Makes 6 to 8 servings

I never thought I'd be a mom who had to sneak vegetables into her kids' food, but here I am, with picky toddlers who only want to eat mac and cheese. Fortunately, this "cheesy" sauce contains a healthy dose of carrots (and gives it that retro orange color) and nutritional yeast for a B_{12} boost.

8 ounces carrots, cut into 1-inch chunks
1/2 medium onion, quartered
16 ounces elbow macaroni
1/2 cup raw cashews
2 cups plain unsweetened almond milk
1/2 cup nutritional yeast
1/4 cup plus 1 teaspoon olive oil, divided
1 tablespoon white miso paste
1 tablespoon Dijon mustard
1 teaspoon salt
1 teaspoon lemon juice
1/2 teaspoon smoked paprika
1/4 teaspoon liquid smoke
4 slices Tempeh Bacon (page 19)

Bring 1 quart of water to a boil in a medium pot. Add the carrots and onion, cover and simmer for 20 minutes until the vegetables are soft. Drain. While the vegetables are cooking, bring 4 quarts of water to a boil in a large pot. Add the macaroni and cook, stirring occasionally, for 8 to 10 minutes, or until the macaroni is al dente. Drain and set aside.

Pulse the cashews in a high-speed blender until finely ground and powdery. Add the cooked carrots and onion to the blender, then add the milk, nutritional yeast, 1/4 cup of the oil, miso paste, mustard, salt, lemon juice, smoked paprika, and liquid smoke. Blend until very smooth.

In a small skillet, heat the remaining 1 teaspoon of oil over medium-high heat. Add the Tempeh Bacon and cook for 5 minutes, turning once, or until browned on both sides. Remove the bacon from the skillet and crumble or chop into smaller pieces. In a large serving dish, combine the macaroni, smoky cheese sauce, and bacon, and mix well until the macaroni is evenly coated.

Note: If you don't have a high-speed blender, you can use a food processor, but the sauce won't be as smooth.

Bacon-Wrapped Mushroom Scallops

Makes 2 to 4 servings

The king trumpet mushroom makes an appearance here—not in bacon form, but as an alternative to scallops. The thick, meaty mushroom stems are sliced to resemble scallops, then marinated and are wrapped in salty, smoky Tempeh Bacon slices. These make a great appetizer or main dish and are delicious as is or wrapped in small Bibb lettuce leaves.

Scallops:

2 sheets sushi nori, torn into 2-inch pieces
2 cups hot water
1/2 teaspoon lemon juice
1/4 teaspoon garlic powder
4 to 6 large king trumpet mushroom stems, about 1 inch wide, cut into
    1-inch rounds (about 16 pieces)
16 slices Tempeh Bacon (page 19)
Olive oil, for drizzling
Smoked paprika, for garnish

Sriracha Bacon Mayo:

1 cup vegan mayonnaise
2 tablespoons Sriracha sauce
1 1/2 teaspoons lime juice
2 tablespoons Baconish Bits (page 32)

Scallops: Combine the nori, hot water, lemon juice, and garlic powder in a large bowl. Steep the nori for 20 minutes, then strain through a fine mesh colander. Reserve the water and discard the nori.

Place the mushroom slices in a large bowl. Pour the strained broth over the mushrooms. Marinate for at least 20 minutes, then drain. While the mushrooms are marinating, preheat the broiler to its highest setting. Line a small baking sheet with parchment paper.

Wrap a slice of bacon around each scallop and secure with a toothpick. You want the tempeh slice to overlap about 1-inch to secure the pick, then trim off the rest of the tempeh for another use. Place the wrapped mushrooms on the baking sheet and drizzle with the oil, then lightly sprinkle with the smoked paprika. Broil for 15 minutes.

Sriracha Bacon Mayo: Mix the mayonnaise, Sriracha, lime juice, and Baconish Bits together in a small bowl. Serve the scallops hot with Sriracha Bacon Mayo.

Chocolate-Peanut Bacon Truffles (page 185)

Sweets and Such

· ·

Don't think that just because there are desserts in this chapter that there won't be any bacon. Smoky little bits of bacon can be a great complement even to sweet dishes. We already know how well bacon goes with things like peanut butter, bananas, and maple syrup, but I have three more words for you: Chocolate. Covered. Bacon.

The recipes in this section are great for sharing with company, or just at home with your closest ones. Go on and make those Baconish Spiced Nuts when you're entertaining, so your guests have something to nibble on before they dive into those Elvis Cupcakes.

Elvis Cupcakes

Makes 12 cupcakes

. . . .

What's better than a "More-to-Love Elvis" Sandwich (page 114)? An Elvis Cupcake, of course! Super moist, fluffy banana cake with a rich, peanut buttery frosting, topped with coconut bacon flakes. Bake these for someone you love, and they'll say, "Thank ya, thank ya very much."

Cupcakes:

1 1/2 cups unbleached all-purpose flour
1/2 cup sugar
1/4 cup brown sugar
1 teaspoon baking powder
1/2 teaspoon baking soda
1/2 cup coconut oil (melted)
4 very ripe medium bananas, mashed with a fork
1/2 cup plain or vanilla vegan yogurt
1/2 teaspoon vanilla extract

Frosting:

8 ounces vegan cream cheese
3/4 cup creamy no-stir peanut butter
2 cups confectioners' sugar
2 tablespoons plain unsweetened almond milk
1/4 cup Coconut Bacon (page 21), for topping
12 dehydrated, sweetened banana chips

Preheat the oven to 350°F. Line a muffin pan with 12 cupcake liners.

Cupcakes: Whisk together the flour, sugar, brown sugar, baking powder, and baking soda in a large bowl. In another medium bowl, combine the oil, bananas, yogurt, and vanilla, and mix until smooth. Add the wet ingredients to the dry ingredients. Mix well.

Pour the batter into the prepared cupcake liners. Each cupcake well should be about 3/4 full.

Bake for 25 to 30 minutes, until golden brown. If you insert a toothpick into the center of one, it should come out clean. Remove the cupcakes from the oven and set aside to cool.

Frosting: While the cupcakes are cooling, prepare the frosting. In a large bowl, cream together the cream cheese and peanut butter with an electric mixer. Alternate adding 1 cup of the confectioners' sugar and 1 tablespoon of the milk, mixing well between each addition. I found that 2 cups of confectioners' sugar is plenty, but add up to 3 cups if you like it sweeter or if it is not thick enough.

When the cupcakes are cooled, generously top them with the frosting. Sprinkle the top with about 1 teaspoon of Coconut Bacon, and place a banana chip in the frosting

Note: You want the bananas to be very ripe. Mostly covered with dark brown spots is perfect. The riper the banana, the moister the cake and the deeper the banana flavor.

Peanut Butter Bacon Cookies
Makes 2 dozen

. . . .

The classic peanut butter cookie is pretty hard to beat . . . until you add a little baconish flavor to it. These cookies are soft and chewy, just the way I like them, and are perfect with a glass of your favorite vegan milk.

1 1/4 cup unbleached all-purpose flour
1/2 teaspoon baking soda
1/2 teaspoon salt
1/2 teaspoon ground cinnamon
1/2 cup smooth peanut butter
1/2 cup vegan butter, melted
1/4 cup sugar
2/3 cup brown sugar
3 tablespoons aquafaba (page 8)
3/4 teaspoon vanilla extract
1 to 2 tablespoons plain unsweetened almond or soy milk
1/4 cup Baconish Bits (page 32)

Preheat the oven to 350°F. Line 2 large baking sheets with parchment paper.

In a large bowl, whisk together the flour, baking soda, salt, and cinnamon.

In a standing mixer with the paddle attachment, mix together the peanut butter and melted butter. Mix in the sugar, brown sugar, aquafaba, and vanilla. Add flour about 1/2 cup at a time, waiting until it is incorporated before adding more. Stop the mixer to scrape the sides as necessary. If you find that the dough is too crumbly and not holding together well, mix in up to 2 tablespoons of nondairy milk. When all the flour is mixed in, fold in the Baconish Bits.

For each cookie, scoop out 1 rounded tablespoon and shape into a ball with your hands. Place it on the baking sheet and lightly flatten it out with your fingers. Bake the cookies 12 minutes (for a soft-baked texture) to 14 minutes (for a crisper cookie), until golden brown, then allow to cool on racks.

Coconut Panna Cotta

with SALTED MAPLE-CARAMEL SAUCE

Makes 4 servings

. . . .

This is an elegant dessert that is actually quite quick and easy to make. Traditional panna cotta is made with gelatin, which is wholly unnecessary when you can use seaweed-derived agar for the same purpose of gelling.

Panna cotta:

1 (13.5-ounce) can full-fat coconut milk

1/2 cup maple syrup

1/4 cup brown sugar

1/2 teaspoon vanilla extract

1 teaspoon agar powder

Salted Maple-Caramel Sauce:

1/2 cup maple syrup

2 tablespoons vegan butter

1/4 teaspoon salt

1/4 teaspoon vanilla extract

Coconut Bacon (page 21) or Chocolate-Covered Coconut Bacon (page 191), for garnish

Panna Cotta: Heat the coconut milk in a small saucepan over medium heat until it is hot but not simmering. Whisk in the maple syrup, brown sugar, and vanilla. Slowly whisk in the agar powder, making sure to break up any lumps. Cook over medium-low heat, whisking occasionally, for 10 minutes. Divide the mixture evenly into 4 ramekins and cool on the counter until they stop steaming. Refrigerate the panna cotta for at least 30 minutes, until firmly set.

Sauce: Whisk the maple syrup, butter, salt, and vanilla together in a small saucepan over medium-high heat. Bring to a boil, then reduce to a simmer for 8 to 10 minutes, until the sauce has thickened and reduced slightly.

To serve, invert each ramekin over a dessert plate. The panna cottas should pop out very easily (if they don't, simply run a knife around the edge of the ramekins to loosen them). Spoon the Salted Maple-Caramel Sauce over the top, and garnish with the Coconut Bacon.

Chocolate-Peanut Bacon Truffles
Makes 28 truffles

Peanut butter. Chocolate. Baconish Bits. These are like a grownup version of peanut butter cups. They are surprisingly easy to make and super fun to box up and give as gifts.

1/2 cup smooth peanut butter
2 tablespoons vegan butter, melted
3/4 cup confectioners' sugar
2 tablespoons Baconish Bits (page 32)
2/3 cup vegan chocolate chips
Additional Baconish Bits and/or Coconut Bacon (page 21), for garnish

Line a large baking sheet with parchment paper. Use an electric mixer to combine the peanut butter, melted butter, and confectioners' sugar. Fold in the Baconish Bits. Scoop out 1 teaspoon of the mixture, roll into a ball with your hands, and place the ball on the prepared baking sheet. Repeat this process with the remaining mixture. Chill in the refrigerator for 20 minutes.

Place the chocolate chips in a medium microwave-safe bowl and microwave in 30-second intervals, stirring between intervals, until melted, about 1 1/2 to 2 minutes.

Dip the peanut butter balls in the melted chocolate. I find it easiest to use 2 small dessert forks to roll the balls in the chocolate and then lift them out, letting the excess chocolate drip back into the bowl. Place the truffles back on the parchment sheet. Sprinkle a few Baconish Bits or place a flake of Coconut Bacon on top of each truffle while the chocolate is still warm.

Chill the truffles in the refrigerator another 20 minutes to set the chocolate. Keep refrigerated until ready to eat—the truffles will soften and melt if left out too long.

Bacon and Cashew Caramel Corn
Makes about 12 cups

This is another great snack mix, perfect for entertaining or, you know, just hanging out at home watching Netflix because you have two very small kids and you're exhausted by 9 p.m. and who has time to clean the house for company anyway?

2/3 cup agave nectar

1/4 cup maple syrup

1/4 cup sugar

2 tablespoons vegan butter

1/2 teaspoon vanilla extract

1/2 teaspoon salt

10 cups popped popcorn (1 microwave bag or 1/2 cup popcorn kernels)

1 cup roasted and salted cashews

1 cup Coconut Bacon (page 21)

Preheat the oven to 300°F. Line a large baking sheet with parchment paper.

In a small, heavy-bottom saucepan, bring the agave, maple syrup, sugar, and butter to a boil. Reduce the heat and simmer 3 to 4 minutes. Remove from the heat and stir in the vanilla and salt.

Combine the popcorn, cashews, and Coconut Bacon in a large mixing bowl. Pour the caramel syrup all over the popcorn mixture, and then mix thoroughly until evenly coated.

Spread the caramel corn in an even layer on the prepared baking sheet. Bake the caramel corn for 15 minutes, then allow to cool. Break up large clumps before serving.

Note: To make your own stovetop popcorn for this recipe, combine 1 tablespoon vegetable oil with 1/2 cup popcorn kernels in a large, heavy-bottom saucepan. Cover with a lid but keep it slightly ajar, so that the steam can escape. Cook, shaking the pan occasionally, over medium heat until the popping starts to slow down, about 5 minutes. Remove from the heat and keep covered another minute until the popping stops.

Miss Piggy Strawberry Ice Cream (page 189)

Maple-Pecan Sundae (page 190)

Nearly-Instant Elvis Ice Cream (page 192)

Miss Piggy Strawberry Ice Cream

with CHOCOLATE-COVERED BACON

Makes about 2 pints

. . . .

We used to live across the street from a very popular ice cream shop called Ample Hills. They only had one or two vegan flavors, like their Coconut Fudge, but wow, were they good. One of the popular specials they had was the (nonvegan) Miss Piggy flavor: strawberry-studded ice cream with candied bacon, which served as the inspiration for this recipe. I don't know how it measures up against their version, but this is delicious, and much kinder to the pigs and cows.

1/4 cup aquafaba (page 8)
1/2 cup confectioners' sugar
1 (14-ounce) can coconut cream (see Note)
1 cup fresh strawberries, trimmed and halved
1 teaspoon vanilla extract
1/2 cup Chocolate-Covered Coconut Bacon (page 191)

Using an electric stand mixer, whip the aquafaba into a meringue, about 10 minutes, until stiff peaks form. Slowly add the confectioners' sugar (the meringue might deflate slightly, but keep mixing until the stiff peaks reappear.)

Combine the coconut cream, strawberries, and vanilla in a bowl and stir to mix well. Add the coconut cream mixture to the meringue and gently stir to combine, keeping as much air in the mixture as possible.

Freeze the ice cream for 3 to 4 hours, or until semi-solid. Fold in the Chocolate-Covered Coconut Bacon. Freeze the ice cream another 2 to 3 hours, or until firm.

Note: Look for Trader Joe's brand coconut cream or other brands, such as Native Forest or Thai Kitchen, in natural food stores or in the Asian or Latin American sections of supermarkets. If you can't find coconut cream, use the solids from 2 (13.5-ounce) cans of full-fat coconut milk that have been refrigerated overnight and not stirred or shaken before opening.

Maple-Pecan Sundaes

with COCONUT BACON

Makes 6 to 8 servings

. . . .

Bean juice in ice cream? I know it sounds weird, but you're going to have to trust me on this one. It's not that weird when you consider that traditional ice cream has egg in the base, and we use aquafaba as an egg replacer. All traces of the bean flavor disappear, and when you taste how light, airy, and smooth it makes this ice cream, you will be convinced of the genius of aquafaba! Even better, you don't even need an ice cream maker! (See photo on page 188.)

Ice cream:
1/4 cup aquafaba (page 8)
1/2 cup confectioners' sugar
1 (14-ounce) can coconut cream (see note)
3/4 cup maple syrup
1/2 cup toasted pecan pieces

Maple-pecan topping:
1/2 cup maple syrup
1/4 cup brown sugar
1 tablespoon vegan butter
2 teaspoons cornstarch mixed with 2 teaspoons hot water
1/2 teaspoon vanilla extract
1/2 cup lightly toasted pecans, chopped
Vegan whipped cream, for serving
Coconut Bacon (page 21), for serving

Ice cream: Use an electric stand mixer to whip the aquafaba into a meringue, about 10 minutes, until stiff peaks form. Slowly add the confectioners' sugar (the meringue might deflate slightly, but keep mixing until the stiff peaks reappear).

Combine the coconut cream and maple syrup in a bowl and stir to mix well. Add the coconut cream mixture to the meringue and gently stir to combine, keeping as much air in the mixture as possible. Place the ice cream in an airtight container and freeze about 3 hours, until it is semi-solid. Fold the pecan pieces into the ice cream, then return the ice cream to the freezer for another 3 to 4 hours, or until firm.

Topping: Bring the maple syrup, brown sugar, and butter to a boil in a small saucepan. When it begins to boil, lower the heat and simmer for 2 minutes. Stir in the cornstarch mixture, return to a boil, then simmer again 3 minutes, stirring often. Remove the topping from the heat, then stir in the vanilla and chopped pecans. Let the topping cool until it is warm or at room temperature. The sauce will continue to thicken as it cools. Store in an airtight container in the refrigerator for up to 2 weeks.

To assemble the sundaes, scoop the ice cream into dessert bowls. Top with the maple-pecan topping, vegan whipped cream, and Coconut Bacon. If the topping hardens, reheat it in the microwave or on the stovetop until it is a pourable consistency again.

Note: Look for Trader Joe's brand coconut cream or other brands, such as Native Forest or Thai Kitchen, in natural food stores or in the Asian or Latin American sections of supermarkets. If you can't find coconut cream, use the solids from 2 (13.5-ounce) cans of full-fat coconut milk that have been refrigerated overnight and not stirred or shaken before opening.

Chocolate-Covered Coconut Bacon
Makes about 1 cup

It's chocolate and coconut bacon. Need I say more?

1/2 cup vegan chocolate chips
1 cup Coconut Bacon (page 21)

Line a large rimmed baking sheet with parchment paper. Place the chocolate chips in a microwave-safe bowl (I use a 1 1/2-quart glass bowl). Microwave in 30-second intervals, stirring with a rubber spatula between intervals, until melted, about 1 1/2 minutes.

Stir in the Coconut Bacon, mix thoroughly and break up any large clumps. Spread the Chocolate-Covered Coconut Bacon on the prepared baking sheet in an even layer and refrigerate 15 minutes to harden.

Nearly-Instant Elvis Ice Cream

Makes 4 servings

I always keep a bag of bananas in the freezer to make smoothies. If you have frozen bananas and a food processor, you can have rich, creamy banana "ice cream" in mere minutes. It's like magic! Once you know how easy it is to make the banana base, you can add anything you want to it, but this Elvis combination is a big hit. (See photo page 188.)

4 frozen medium bananas, broken into chunks
1/4 cup creamy or crunchy peanut butter
2 tablespoons Coconut Bacon (page 21), plus more for topping
Crushed peanuts for topping, optional
Vegan whipped cream, optional

Place the frozen banana chunks in a food processor. Blend for a few minutes (it will be crumbly at first, so you may have to stop and scrape down the sides a few times). Keep processing, and after a few minutes, it will suddenly become the texture of soft-serve ice cream. At this point, mix in the peanut butter and Coconut Bacon.

Transfer the ice cream to dessert dishes and top with the additional Coconut Bacon, crushed peanuts, and vegan whipped cream, if desired.

Bacon-Wrapped Dates

Makes 4 servings

These sweet and savory little bites are easy to make, perfect hors d'oeuvres when you're having company. (See photo page 194.)

    12 dried Medjool dates
    24 roasted salted almonds
    12 slices Tempeh Bacon (page 19)
    Olive oil, for brushing

Preheat the oven to 400°F. Line a baking sheet with parchment paper.

Use a sharp paring knife to split each date halfway through lengthwise. Stuff each date with 2 almonds, then wrap a slice of Tempeh Bacon around it and secure with a toothpick. You want about a 1-inch overlap of Tempeh Bacon in order to be able to secure it. Trim off the remaining bacon and use in a tofu scramble or other recipe.

Brush a small amount of oil over the bacon and place on the parchment paper. Bake for 12 minutes. Serve warm or room temperature.

Baconish Spiced Nuts

Makes about 2 cups

These nuts are sweet, salty, spicy, and totally addictive. They are a big crowd pleaser!

2 tablespoons aquafaba (page 8)
1/2 teaspoon salt
2 cups roasted and salted cashews, peanuts, or any combination of nuts
2 tablespoons brown sugar
1 tablespoon maple syrup
3/4 teaspoon cayenne
1/2 teaspoon dried thyme
1/4 teaspoon ground cinnamon
1/4 teaspoon ground cumin
1/2 cup Coconut Bacon (page 21)

Preheat the oven to 350°F. Line a baking sheet with parchment paper.

In a bowl, combine the aquafaba and salt and whisk until foamy. Add the nuts and toss to coat. Add the brown sugar, maple syrup, cayenne, thyme, cinnamon, and cumin. Toss to coat.

Spread the nuts evenly on the prepared baking sheet in a single layer. Bake the nuts for 15 minutes, stirring halfway through. Let the nuts cool on the sheet. Add the Coconut Bacon, mixing and breaking up any large clumps. Serve. Store any leftover nuts in an airtight container at room temperature up to 1 week.

Sweet and Savory Bacon Jam
Makes about 1 1/2 cups

. . . .

This is a sweet, tangy condiment with just the right hint of baconishness. Top your veggie burgers with it, put it inside your vegan grilled cheese sandwiches, slather it on biscuits. It just may become your new favorite condiment.

> 4 tablespoons olive oil, divided
> 6 ounces Tempeh Bacon (page 19), coarsely chopped
> 1 heaping cup coarsely chopped onion (about 1 medium onion)
> 3/4 cup coarsely chopped shallots (about 2 large shallots)
> 2 cloves garlic, minced
> 1/3 cup maple syrup
> 1/4 cup brown sugar
> 1/4 cup apple cider vinegar
> 2 tablespoons whole-grain mustard
> 1/2 teaspoon ground ginger

Heat 2 tablespoons of the oil in a medium skillet over medium-high heat. Add the bacon pieces and cook until dark brown and crisp, about 6 minutes, stirring frequently to avoid sticking. Remove the bacon from the skillet and set aside.

Heat the remaining 2 tablespoons of oil in the same skillet. Add the onion, shallots, and garlic, and cook until soft and translucent, 8 to 10 minutes. Stir frequently, scraping up as much of the browned bits from the bottom of the skillet as you can.

Add the bacon back to the skillet. Stir in the maple syrup, brown sugar, apple cider vinegar, mustard, and ginger. Reduce the heat to low and simmer 15 minutes, until the mixture has reduced and become very thick and jammy. Remove the jam from the heat and let cool about 10 minutes.

Transfer the mixture to a food processor and pulse 4 to 5 times, or until it reaches the desired consistency. Sweet and Savory Bacon Jam will keep several weeks refrigerated in an airtight container.

Need More Vegan Bacon?

Look, sometimes you're not feeling very DIY, but you're craving vegan bacon. Here is a list of some vegan bacon products that are already out there, just waiting to be BLT'd.

Augason Farms Bacon Flavored Bits – I'm not sure why these gigantic 2-pound tubs of bacon-flavored bits are labeled "emergency food" at places like Walmart, but when the zombie apocalypse happens I guess you should have these stocked in your hideout shelter.

Betty Crocker Bac-Os Bits – These fall into the "accidentally vegan" category. Not exactly healthy, but they are relatively easy to find and are free of animal products.

CocoBacon – Made by Coconut Organics, this is a deliciously seasoned coconut bacon, with a hint of sweetness.

Dang Toasted Coconut Chips (Savory Bacon flavor) – It's a personal pet peeve of mine when people say "dang," but I'll forgive them because they make tasty coconut bacon.

Frontier Bac'Uns – Relatively easy to find in grocery and health food stores, these have a very smoky flavor.

J&D's Bacon Croutons – These are great not just on salads but also in soups, stuffings, or crushed up and used as breading.

J&D's Bacon Rub – This spice blend makes everything taste baconish. Rub it on your tofu or on vegetables before roasting them.

J&D's Bacon Salt – Another great seasoning blend from J&D's, their Bacon Salt comes in a wide variety of smoke flavors. Sprinkle it on vegetables, popcorn, just about anything you can imagine.

Jim Beam Bacon Mustard – Add it to your veggie dogs and burgers. Yum.

Kettle Brand Maple Bacon Potato Chips – These potato chips are addictively sweet, salty, and smoky. Because sometimes you need bacon-y potato chips, you know?

Late July Bacon Habanero Tortilla Chips – These are really good, sweet-smoky chips, but don't expect them to be hot. There's no heat, despite having habanero in their name.

Let Thy Food Chedd'r Bac'n Dip – This incredibly versatile dip is cheesy and smoky. Pour it on nachos, baked potatoes, burgers, pasta, vegetables, or, you know, just dip your chips in it.

Lightlife Organic Fakin' Bacon Tempeh Strips – These tempeh strips are perfectly seasoned and smoky. One of my favorites.

Lightlife Smart Bacon – Packaged strips made from soy and wheat gluten. Decent smoky flavor, but I find they tend to dry out and overcook easily.

Louisville Vegan Jerky Co. Maple Bacon Jerky – This company makes the best vegan jerky I've ever had. Good enough to fool meat eaters.

Louisville Vegan Jerky Co. Unreal Bacon Bits – These aren't your average bacon bits. They're more like mini chunks of bacon-flavored jerky. Really good.

McCormick Bac'n Pieces – Artificially flavored and containing a bunch of not-so-healthy ingredients, these are easy to find pretty much anywhere. They are technically vegan, although really not good for you in any other way.

Organic Matters Vegan Bacon Bits – This is another brand of packaged coconut bacon; it is smoky, salty, and very tasty.

Phoney Baloney's Coconut Bacon – Probably the best-known brand of coconut bacon, there are a few different varieties of it, including a soy-free and low-sodium version.

Rescue Chocolate Fakin' Bacon! – Eat chocolate and help save animals at the same time! This is one of my favorite chocolate companies—all the products are vegan and 100 percent of the profits go to various animal welfare organizations. This dreamy dark chocolate bar is studded with smoky bacon-y bits.

RITZ Crackers (bacon flavor) – These also fall into the accidentally vegan category, but don't worry—I won't judge you for loving them.

Stonewall's Jerquee (Country Bacon flavor) – People seem to either love or hate this brand of vegan jerky. I fall into the . . . well, I-don't-love-it category.

Sweet Earth Benevolent Bacon – These seitan strips taste really good. I wouldn't say they remind me very much of bacon, but they're really good.

The Good Bean BBQ Bacon Bean Chips – These were one of my favorite discoveries. They are truly delicious and made from a blend of chickpeas, navy beans, red lentils, pea protein, sweet potatoes, and red quinoa. So now, when an annoying person asks you where you get your protein, you can answer, "From BBQ Bacon Bean Chips, of course."

Tofurky Smoky Maple Bacon Marinated Tempeh – Another brand of tempeh bacon, these taste good but are shorter in length than the Lightlife strips, which makes them harder to use for bacon-wrapped recipes.

Upton Naturals Bacon Seitan – This is the best store-bought seitan bacon I have found. It has good seasoning and texture. Also, in addition to their vegan bacon, Upton Naturals now offers pig-friendly Chili Lime Carnitas Jackfruit and Bar-B-Que Jackfruit.

Urban Kitchen Maple Bacon Granola – A little sweet, a little smoky, it can be eaten as is, sprinkled on some vegan yogurt, or mixed into the topping of a fruit crumble for a baconish twist on dessert.

Vegan Magic – You'll never guess what this stuff is. Vegan bacon grease! You read that right. Made from coconut oil and bacon-y seasonings, this stuff is crazy good. There are endless uses for it: fry your pancakes in it, sauté all your veggies with it, make a grilled cheese with it, bake your biscuits with it. Seriously, if you want to take any of my baconish recipes to the next level, replace all or part of the oil or buttery spread with this. It really is magic.

Wayfare Pig Out Bacony Bits – This is a great soy-free version of vegan bacon bits.

Yves Canadian Bacon Slices – These slices are great and perfect for vegan "eggs" Benedict.

Acknowledgments

There are several people I have to thank for their help, encouragement, and support.

Thank you to my publisher, Jon Robertson, for giving me this incredible opportunity.

Many thanks to Andrea and Mark Huntley for your very generous tech support and for never openly laughing at how computer challenged I am. A million vegan doughnuts cannot thank you enough.

Thank you to Wendy Edwards, for your friendship, contribution, and support of this book idea from the very earliest stages.

Thank you to Susanne Cerha for your willingness to lend your creative design brilliance any time I asked for it.

Many thanks to Barent, Maria, and Cyla, for being my most trusted taste testers, leftover cleaner-uppers, and for your incredible friendship and support for this book.

Thank you to Valerie Oula for being a trusted tester and for always sending energy and light.

Thank you to Leanne Hilgart for being the sweetest boss in the world. I never could have finished this project without such an accommodating schedule.

Thank you to all the vegan bloggers and cookbook authors who amaze and inspire me every day with your culinary awesomeness and creativity.

And thank you to my husband, Anthony, for all your help in bringing this project to life and making it look so beautiful.

About the Author

Leinana Two Moons is the author of the blog *Vegan Good Things.* Her writing and photography have appeared in *LAIKA* and *VegNews* magazines. A longtime vegan, she is dedicated to creating recipes that are satisfying enough to please anyone, vegan, vegetarian, flexitarian, or hardcore carnivore alike. She is active in the New York City vegan community and lives in Brooklyn, New York, with her husband and two children, who are all vegan. *Baconish* is her first cookbook.

Sweet and Savory Bacon Jam (page 196)

Index

The author with a friend at Woodstock Farm Animal Sanctuary.

Metric Conversions and Equivalents

The recipes in this book have not been tested with metric measurements, so some variations may occur.

LIQUID

U.S.	METRIC
1 tsp	5 ml
1 tbs	15 ml
2 tbs	30 ml
1/4 cup	60 ml
1/3 cup	75 ml
1/2 cup	120 ml
2/3 cup	150 ml
3/4 cup	180 ml
1 cup	240 ml
1 1/4 cups	300 ml
1 1/3 cups	325 ml
1 1/2 cups	350 ml
1 2/3 cups	375 ml
1 3/4 cups	400 ml
2 cups (1 pint)	475 ml
3 cups	720 ml
4 cups (1 quart)	945 ml

LENGTH

U.S.	Metric
1/2 inch	1.25 cm
1 inch	2.5 cm
6 inches	15 cm
8 inches	20 cm
10 inches	25 cm
12 inches	30 cm

GENERAL METRIC CONVERSION FORMULAS

Ounces to grams	ounces x 28.35 = grams
Grams to ounces	grams x 0.035 = ounces
Pounds to grams	pounds x 435.5 = grams
Pounds to kilograms	pounds x 0.45 = kilograms
Cups to liters	cups x 0.24 = liters
Fahrenheit to Celsius	(°F - 32) x 5 ÷ 9 = °C
Celsius to Fahrenheit	(°C x 9) ÷ 5 + 32 = °F

WEIGHT

U.S.	METRIC
1/2 oz	14 g
1 oz	28 g
1 1/2 oz	43 g
2 oz	57 g
21/2 oz	71 g
4 oz	113 g
5 oz	142 g
6 oz	170 g
7 oz	200 g
8 oz (1/2 lb)	227 g
9 oz	255 g
10 oz	284 g
11 oz	312 g
12 oz	340 g
13 oz	368 g
14 oz	400 g
15 oz	425 g
16 oz (1 lb)	454 g

OVEN TEMPERATURE

°F	Gas Mark	°C
250	1/2	120
275	1	140
300	2	150
325	3	165
350	4	180
375	5	190
400	6	200
425	7	220
450	8	230
475	9	240
500	10	260
550	Broil	290

Maple-Bacon Doughnuts (page 68)